Amazon Polly Developer Guide

A catalogue record for this book is available from the Hong Kong Public Libraries.

Published in Hong Kong by Samurai Media Limited.

Email: info@samuraimedia.org

ISBN 9789888408740

Contents

What Is Amazon Polly?

Amazon Polly is a cloud service that converts text into lifelike speech. You can use Amazon Polly to develop applications that increase engagement and accessibility. Amazon Polly supports multiple languages and includes a variety of lifelike voices, so you can build speech-enabled applications that work in multiple locations and use the ideal voice for your customers. With Amazon Polly, you only pay for the text you synthesize. You can also cache and replay Amazon Polly's generated speech at no additional cost.

Common use cases for Amazon Polly include, but are not limited to, mobile applications such as newsreaders, games, eLearning platforms, accessibility applications for visually impaired people, and the rapidly growing segment of Internet of Things (IoT).

Amazon Polly is not certified for use with regulated workloads such as Payment Card Industry (PCI) Data Security Standard (DSS), HIPAA (Health Insurance Portability and Accountability Act of 1996), or FedRAMP.

Some of the benefits of using Amazon Polly include:

- **High quality** – Amazon Polly uses best-in-class Text-to-Speech (TTS) technology to synthesize natural speech with high pronunciation accuracy (including abbreviations, acronym expansions, date/time interpretations, and homograph disambiguation).

- **Low latency** – Amazon Polly ensures fast response times, which make it a viable option for low-latency use cases such as dialog systems.

- **Support for a large portfolio of languages and voices** – Amazon Polly supports dozens of voices and multiple languages, offering male and female voice options for most languages.

- **Cost-effective** – Amazon Polly's pay-per-use model means there are no setup costs. You can start small and scale up as your application grows.

- **Cloud-based solution** – On-device Text-to-Speech solutions require significant computing resources, notably CPU power, RAM, and disk space. These can result in higher development costs and higher power consumption on devices such as tablets, smart phones, etc. In contrast, Text-to-Speech conversion done in the cloud dramatically reduces local resource requirements. This enables support of all the available languages and voices at the best possible quality. Moreover, speech improvements are instantly available to all end-users and do not require additional updates for devices.

Are You a First-time User of Amazon Polly?

If you are a first-time user of Amazon Polly, we recommend that you read the following sections in the listed order:

1. **Amazon Polly: How It Works** – This section introduces various Amazon Polly inputs and options that you can work with in order to create an end-to-end experience.

2. **Getting Started with Amazon Polly** – In this section, you set up your account and test Amazon Polly speech synthesis.

3. **Example Applications** – This section provides additional examples that you can use to explore Amazon Polly.

Amazon Polly: How It Works

Amazon Polly converts input text into life-like speech. You just need to call the `SynthesizeSpeech` method, provide the text you wish to synthesize, select one of the available Text-to-Speech (TTS) voices, and specify an audio output format. Amazon Polly then synthesizes the provided text into a high-quality speech audio stream.

- **Input text** – Provide the text you want to synthesize, and Amazon Polly returns an audio stream. You can provide the input as plain text or in Speech Synthesis Markup Language (SSML) format. With SSML you can control various aspects of speech such as pronunciation, volume, pitch, and speech rate. For more information, see Using SSML.

- **Available voices** – Amazon Polly provides a portfolio of multiple languages and a variety of voices. For most languages you can select from several different voices, including both male and female. You only need to specify the voice name when calling the `SynthesizeSpeech` operation, and then the service uses this voice to convert the text to speech. Amazon Polly is not a translation service—the synthesized speech is in the language of the text. Numbers using digits (for example, *53*, not *fifty-three*) are synthesized in the language of the voice.

- **Output format** – Amazon Polly can deliver the synthesized speech in multiple formats. You can select the audio format that suits your needs. For example, you might request the speech in the MP3 or Ogg Vorbis format to consume in web and mobile applications. Or, you might request the PCM output format for AWS IoT devices and telephony solutions.

What's Next?

If you are new to Amazon Polly, we recommend that you to read the following topics in order:

- Getting Started with Amazon Polly
- Example Applications
- Limits in Amazon Polly

Common Questions

This topic provides answers to questions that are commonly asked about Amazon Polly.

- General Questions
- Content Rendering
- Voices
- Data Security and Confidentiality

General Questions

Q: Can I save the synthesized speech?

You can save the output of the synthesis for use on your own system. You can also call Amazon Polly, and then encrypt the file with any encryption key and store it in Amazon Simple Storage Service (Amazon S3) or any other secure storage. The Amazon Polly `SynthesizeSpeech` call is stateless and is not associated with a customer identity. You can't retrieve it from Amazon Polly later.

Content Rendering

Q: Some of my text coming out with the stress on the wrong syllable when it is spoken by Amazon Polly. I've even tried using an acute accent (U+0301) to mark the stress but it is still on the wrong syllable. How can I fix this?

Amazon Polly doesn't currently recognize an acute accent (U+0301) as indicating syllable stress in a word. However, there are two ways you can change the stress in a word. You can use an IPA phone and ssml tags to alter the pronunciation of the word. For more information, see SSML Tags in Amazon Polly. In some languages, you can also use an apostrophe immediately after the syllable to indicate a change in stress. For instance, in Russian, the words′ and′ have different stresses (marked here with an acute accent). However, because of the identical spelling, Amazon Polly will pronounce them both with the stress on the final syllable, according to standard language usage. You can use an apostrophe to mark the alternatively stressed syllable, as in ′, and the Amazon Polly will stress the correct syllable.

Q: When I use bullet points in my text, Amazon Polly doesn't render them correctly. It says "minus" every time it encounters one. What do I do?

If you use "-" (a hyphen) as a substitute for a bullet point, in some languages,Amazon Polly renders it as a minus sign. If you want to use hyphens as substitutes for a bullet point, you can do so with a lexicon entry. For more information, see Managing Lexicons.

Q: I use the "/" (forward slash) symbol frequently in my text, especially when saying "and/or" and "yes/no." How does Amazon Polly render this?

In English, Amazon Polly renders "and/or" in speech as "and or." Currently, this rule isn't available in other languages. In languages other than English, Amazon Polly renders "yes/no" as "yes slash no." If you want to change this behavior, you can use a lexicon entry. For more information, see Managing Lexicons.

Q: When I use text from an existing source in order to synthesize speach using the AWS CLI on a Linux machine, some UTF-8 characters do not seem work with Amazon Polly, even though the same characters seem to work properly using the Console. What is happening?

This is based in how the Unix Shell handles Unicode and isn't a Amazon Polly-specific problem. Two options are available: you can find the problem characters and replace them in the input text, or you can u tilize an alternate means of accessing Amazon Polly that does not experience this issue, such as the PHP interface. This is a known issue that we are working to address and only a few uncommon unicode characters have this issue.

Q: When I try to synthesize text from a source containing International Phonetic Alphabet (IPA) symbols, Amazon Polly doesn't recognize them and even tries to pronounce some of them. How do I fix this?

Amazon Polly does not recognize IPA symbols unless SSML (Speech Synthesis Markup Language) is used to delineate it. However, since small sections of IPA symbols usually indicate a pronunciation guide for a reader, in many cases, this section can be safely removed from the input text by simple deletion. You can also use a lexicon to change the way this is rendered by Amazon Polly. For more information, see Using SSML and Managing Lexicons.

Voices

Q: How can I listen to a voice to see if I want to use it?

You can listen to any voice supported by Amazon Polly by synthesizing a short text through the Amazon Polly console or by using the `synthesize-speech` API with the AWS CLI. You can select any supported voice in the console and listen to the voice by running a sample text. For more information, see Exercise 1: Synthesizing Speech Quick Start (Console). In the AWS CLI, you can use the `voice-id` of the voice you want to hear when you run the `synthesize-speech` API. For more information, see Step 3.2: Getting Started Exercise Using the AWS CLI.

Q: How long will the voices be available? If I choose a voice for my application now, will it still be available in five years?

To ensure continuous support for customers, we don't plan to retire any voices. This applies to both currently available and future voices.

Data Security and Confidentiality

Q: Can I choose to mask certain data fields so that they are not stored?(For instance, if I convert text with some sensitive data, but don't want it stored on the AWS systems, can I mask it?

No. Amazon Polly doesn't currently support this functionality.

Q: The text I want to use with Amazon Polly is confidential. How is my data protected?

All text submissions are protected by Secure Sockets Layer (SSL) while in transit, and are stored using RSA encryption. We keep the service logs and text separate, so that the content can't be linked with the customer ID. As a result, Amazon Polly does not associate text submissions with customer identity.

Q: How long is data retained?

Amazon Polly retains data for 14 days. After that, it's automatically deleted from our system.

Q: Can I request that data be wiped earlier?

Yes, you can request that by contacting AWS Support.

Getting Started with Amazon Polly

Amazon Polly provides simple API operations that you can easily integrate with your existing applications. For a list of supported operations, see Actions. You can use either of the following options:

- AWS SDKs – When using the SDKs, your requests to Amazon Polly are automatically signed and authenticated using the credentials you provide. This is the recommended choice for building your applications.

- AWS CLI – You can use the AWS CLI to access any of Amazon Polly functionality without having to write any code.

The following sections describe how to get set up and provide an introductory exercise.

- Step 1: Set Up an AWS Account and Create a User
- Step 2: Getting Started Using the Console
- Step 3: Getting Started Using the AWS CLI
- What's Next?

Step 1: Set Up an AWS Account and Create a User

Before you use Amazon Polly for the first time, complete the following tasks:

1. Step 1.1: Sign up for AWS

2. Step 1.2: Create an IAM User

Step 1.1: Sign up for AWS

When you sign up for Amazon Web Services (AWS), your AWS account is automatically signed up for all services in AWS, including Amazon Polly. You are charged only for the services that you use.

With Amazon Polly, you pay only for the resources you use. If you are a new AWS customer, you can get started with Amazon Polly for free. For more information, see AWS Free Usage Tier.

If you already have an AWS account, skip to the next step. If you don't have an AWS account, perform the steps in the following procedure to create one.

To create an AWS account

1. Open https://aws.amazon.com/, and then choose **Create an AWS Account**. **Note**
This might be unavailable in your browser if you previously signed into the AWS Management Console. In that case, choose **Sign in to a different account**, and then choose **Create a new AWS account**.

2. Follow the online instructions.

    Part of the sign-up procedure involves receiving a phone call and entering a PIN using the phone keypad.

Note your AWS account ID because you'll need it for the next step.

Step 1.2: Create an IAM User

Services in AWS, such as Amazon Polly, require that you provide credentials when you access them so that the service can determine whether you have permissions to access the resources owned by that service. The console requires your password. You can create access keys for your AWS account to access the AWS CLI or API. However, we don't recommend that you access AWS using the credentials for your AWS account. Instead, we recommend that you use AWS Identity and Access Management (IAM). Create an IAM user, add the user to an IAM group with administrative permissions, and then grant administrative permissions to the IAM user that you created. You can then access AWS using a special URL and that IAM user's credentials.

If you signed up for AWS, but you haven't created an IAM user for yourself, you can create one using the IAM console.

The Getting Started exercises in this guide assume that you have a user (`adminuser`) with administrator privileges. Follow the procedure to create `adminuser` in your account.

To create an administrator user and sign in to the console

1. Create an administrator user called `adminuser` in your AWS account. For instructions, see Creating Your First IAM User and Administrators Group in the *IAM User Guide*.

2. A user can sign in to the AWS Management Console using a special URL. For more information, How Users Sign In to Your Account in the *IAM User Guide*.

Important
The Getting Started exercises use the adminuser credentials. For added security, when building and testing production application we recommend you create a service-specific administrator user who has permissions for only the Amazon Polly actions. For an example policy that grants Amazon Polly specific permissions, see Example 1: Allow All Amazon Polly Actions.

For more information about IAM, see the following:

- AWS Identity and Access Management (IAM)
- Getting Started
- IAM User Guide

Next Step

Step 2: Getting Started Using the Console

Step 2: Getting Started Using the Console

The Amazon Polly console is the easiest way to get started testing and using Amazon Polly's speech synthesizing. The Amazon Polly console supports synthesizing speech from either plain text or SSML input.

- Exercise 1: Synthesizing Speech Quick Start (Console)
- Exercise 2: Synthesizing Speech (Plain Text Input)
- Next Step

Exercise 1: Synthesizing Speech Quick Start (Console)

The Quick Start walks you through the fastest way to test the Amazon Polly speech synthesis for speech quality. When you select the **Text-to-Speech** tab, the text field for entering your text is pre-loaded with example text so you can quickly try out Amazon Polly.

To quickly test Amazon Polly

1. Sign in to the AWS Management Console and open the Amazon Polly console at https://console.aws. amazon.com/polly/.

2. Choose the **Text-to-Speech** tab.

3. (Optional) Choose **SSML**.

4. Choose a language and region, then choose a voice.

5. Choose **Listen to speech**.

For more in-depth testing, see the following topics:

- Exercise 2: Synthesizing Speech (Plain Text Input)

- Using SSML with the Amazon Polly Console

- Applying Lexicons Using the Console (Synthesize Speech)

Exercise 2: Synthesizing Speech (Plain Text Input)

The following procedure synthesizes speech using plain text input. Note how "W3C" and the date "10/3" (October 3rd) are synthesized.

To synthesize speech using plain text input

1. After logging on to the Amazon Polly console, choose **Get started**, and then choose the **Text-to-Speech** tab.

2. Choose the **Plain text** tab.

3. Type or paste this text into the input box.

```
1 He was caught up in the game.
2 In the middle of the 10/3/2014 W3C meeting
3 he shouted, "Score!" quite loudly.
```

4. For **Choose a language and region**, choose **English US**, then choose the voice you want to use for this text.

5. To listen to the speech immediately, choose **Listen to speech**.

6. To save the speech to a file, do one of the following:

    1. Choose **Save speech to MP3**.

2. To change to a different file format, choose **Change file format**, choose the file format you want, and then choose **Change**.

For more in-depth examples, see the following topics:

- Applying Lexicons Using the Console (Synthesize Speech)
- Using SSML with the Amazon Polly Console

Next Step

Step 3: Getting Started Using the AWS CLI

Step 3: Getting Started Using the AWS CLI

Using the AWS CLI you can perform almost all Amazon Polly operations you can perform using the Amazon Polly console. You cannot listen to the synthesized speech using the AWS CLI. Instead, you must save it to a file and then open the file in an application that can play the file.

- Step 3.1: Set Up the AWS Command Line Interface (AWS CLI)
- Step 3.2: Getting Started Exercise Using the AWS CLI

Step 3.1: Set Up the AWS Command Line Interface (AWS CLI)

Follow the steps to download and configure the AWS Command Line Interface (AWS CLI).

Important
You don't need the AWS CLI to perform the steps in this Getting Started exercise. However, some of the exercises in this guide use the AWS CLI. You can skip this step and go to Step 3.2: Getting Started Exercise Using the AWS CLI, and then set up the AWS CLI later when you need it.

To set up the AWS CLI

1. Download and configure the AWS CLI. For instructions, see the following topics in the *AWS Command Line Interface User Guide*:

    - Getting Set Up with the AWS Command Line Interface

    - Configuring the AWS Command Line Interface

2. Add a named profile for the administrator user in the AWS CLI config file. You use this profile when executing the AWS CLI commands. For more information about named profiles, see Named Profiles in the *AWS Command Line Interface User Guide*.

```
1 [profile adminuser]
2     aws_access_key_id = adminuser access key ID
3     aws_secret_access_key = adminuser secret access key
4     region = aws-region
```

For a list of available AWS Regions and those supported by Amazon Polly, see Regions and Endpoints in the *Amazon Web Services General Reference*.

If you specify one of the Amazon Polly supported regions when you configure the AWS CLI, you can omit the following line from the AWS CLI code examples. If you specify a region not supported by Amazon Polly in your AWS CLI configuration (for example, if you're an existing AWS customer using other services in regions that don't support Amazon Polly), you must include the following line:

```
1 --region polly-supported-aws-region
```

3. Verify the setup by typing the following help command at the command prompt:

```
1 aws help
```

A list of valid AWS commands should appear in the AWS CLI window.

To enable Amazon Polly in the AWS CLI (optional)

If you have previously downloaded and configured the AWS CLI, Amazon Polly may not be available without reconfiguring the AWS CLI. This procedure checks to see if this is necessary and provides instructions if Amazon Polly is not automatically available.

1. Verify the availability of Amazon Polly by typing the following help command at the command prompt:

```
1 aws polly help
```

If a description of Amazon Polly and a list of valid commands is displayed, appears in the AWS CLI window. If Amazon Polly is available in the AWS CLI and can be used immediately. In this case, you can skip the remainder of this procedure. If this is not displayed, continue with Step 2.

2. Use one of the two following options to enable Amazon Polly:

    1. Uninstall and reinstall the AWS CLI.

       For instructions, see the following topic in the *AWS Command Line Interface User Guide*: Installing the AWS Command Line Interface.

or

2. Download the file service-2.json.

   At the command prompt, run the following:

   ```
   1 aws configure add-model --service-model file://service-2.json --service-name polly
   ```

3. Reverify the availability of Amazon Polly:

   ```
   1 aws polly help
   ```

   The description of Amazon Polly should be visible.

Next Step

Step 3.2: Getting Started Exercise Using the AWS CLI

Step 3.2: Getting Started Exercise Using the AWS CLI

Now you can test the speech synthesis offered by Amazon Polly. In this exercise, you call the `SynthesizeSpeech` operation by passing in sample text. You can save the resulting audio as a file and verify its content.

If you specified one of the Amazon Polly supported regions when you configured the AWS CLI, you can omit the following line from the AWS CLI code examples. If you specified a region not supported by Amazon Polly in your AWS CLI configuration (for example, if you're an existing AWS customer using other services in regions that don't support Amazon Polly), you must include the following line:

```
1 --region polly-supported-aws-region
```

1. Run the `synthesize-speech` AWS CLI command to synthesize sample text to an audio file (`hello.mp3`).

   The following AWS CLI example is formatted for Unix, Linux, and macOS. For Windows, replace the backslash (\) Unix continuation character at the end of each line with a caret (^) and use full quotation marks (") around the input text with single quotes (') for interior tags.

   ```
   1 aws polly synthesize-speech \
   2     --output-format mp3 \
   3     --voice-id Joanna \
   4     --text 'Hello, my name is Joanna. I learned about the W3C on 10/3 of last year.' \
   5     hello.mp3
   ```

   In the call to `synthesize-speech`, you provide sample text for the synthesis, the voice to use (by providing a voice ID, explained in the following step 3), and the output format. The command saves the resulting audio to the `hello.mp3` file.

   In addition to the MP3 file, the above operation produces the following output to the console.

   ```
   1 {
   2         "ContentType": "audio/mpeg",
   3         "RequestCharacters": "71"
   4 }
   ```

2. Play the resulting `hello.mp3` file to verify the synthesized speech.

3. You can get the list of available voices by using the `DescribeVoices` operation. Run the following `describe-voices` AWS CLI command.

   ```
   1 aws polly describe-voices
   ```

   In response, Amazon Polly returns the list of all available voices. For each voice the response provides the following metadata: voice ID, language code, language name, and the gender of the voice. The following is a sample response:

   ```
   1 {
   2     "Voices": [
   3         {
   4             "Gender": "Female",
   5             "Name": "Salli",
   6             "LanguageName": "US English",
   7             "Id": "Salli",
   8             "LanguageCode": "en-US"
   9         },
   10         {
   11             "Gender": "Female",
   12             "Name": "Joanna",
   13             "LanguageName": "US English",
   ```

```
14            "Id": "Kendra",
15            "LanguageCode": "en-US"
16        }
17    ]
18 }
```

Optionally, you can specify the language code to find the available voices for a specific language. Amazon Polly supports dozens of voices. The following example lists all the voices for Brazilian Portuguese.

```
1 aws polly describe-voices \
2     --language-code pt-BR
```

For a list of language codes, see DescribeVoices. These language codes are W3C language identification tags (*ISO 639 code for the language name-ISO 3166 country code*). For example, en-US (US English), en-GB (British English), and es-ES (Spanish), etc.

You can also use the `help` option in the AWS CLI to get the list of language codes:

```
1 aws polly describe-voices help
```

What's Next?

This guide provides additional examples, some of which are Python code examples that use AWS SDK for Python (Boto) to make API calls to Amazon Polly. We recommend you to set up Python and test the example code provided in the following section. For additional examples, see Example Applications.

Set Up Python and Test an Example

To test the Python example code, you need the AWS SDK for Python (Boto). For instruction, see AWS SDK for Python (Boto3).

To test Example Python Code

The following Python code example does the following:

- Uses the AWS SDK for Python (Boto) to send a `SynthesizeSpeech` request to Amazon Polly (by providing simple text as input).

- Accesses the resulting audio stream in the response and saves the audio to a file on your local disk (speech.mp3).

- Plays the audio file with the default audio player for your local system.

Save the code to a file (example.py) and run it.

```python
1  """Getting Started Example for Python 2.7+/3.3+"""
2  from boto3 import Session
3  from botocore.exceptions import BotoCoreError, ClientError
4  from contextlib import closing
5  import os
6  import sys
7  import subprocess
8  from tempfile import gettempdir
9
10 # Create a client using the credentials and region defined in the [adminuser]
11 # section of the AWS credentials file (~/.aws/credentials).
12 session = Session(profile_name="adminuser")
13 polly = session.client("polly")
14
15 try:
16     # Request speech synthesis
17     response = polly.synthesize_speech(Text="Hello world!", OutputFormat="mp3",
18                                        VoiceId="Joanna")
19 except (BotoCoreError, ClientError) as error:
20     # The service returned an error, exit gracefully
21     print(error)
22     sys.exit(-1)
23
24 # Access the audio stream from the response
25 if "AudioStream" in response:
26     # Note: Closing the stream is important as the service throttles on the
27     # number of parallel connections. Here we are using contextlib.closing to
28     # ensure the close method of the stream object will be called automatically
29     # at the end of the with statement's scope.
30     with closing(response["AudioStream"]) as stream:
31         output = os.path.join(gettempdir(), "speech.mp3")
32
```

```
33          try:
34              # Open a file for writing the output as a binary stream
35              with open(output, "wb") as file:
36                  file.write(stream.read())
37          except IOError as error:
38              # Could not write to file, exit gracefully
39              print(error)
40              sys.exit(-1)
41
42  else:
43      # The response didn't contain audio data, exit gracefully
44      print("Could not stream audio")
45      sys.exit(-1)
46
47  # Play the audio using the platform's default player
48  if sys.platform == "win32":
49      os.startfile(output)
50  else:
51      # the following works on Mac and Linux. (Darwin = mac, xdg-open = linux).
52      opener = "open" if sys.platform == "darwin" else "xdg-open"
53      subprocess.call([opener, output])
```

For additional examples including an example application, see Example Applications.

Speech Marks

The following code sample shows how to use Java-based applications to synthesize speech marks for inputed text. This functionality uses the SynthesizeSpeech API.

For more information on this functionality, see Speech Marks .

For more information on the API, see the reference for http://docs.aws.amazon.com/polly/latest/dg/API_SynthesizeSpeech.html API.

```java
1  package com.amazonaws.polly.samples;
2
3  import com.amazonaws.services.polly.AmazonPolly;
4  import com.amazonaws.services.polly.AmazonPollyClientBuilder;
5  import com.amazonaws.services.polly.model.OutputFormat;
6  import com.amazonaws.services.polly.model.SpeechMarkType;
7  import com.amazonaws.services.polly.model.SynthesizeSpeechRequest;
8  import com.amazonaws.services.polly.model.SynthesizeSpeechResult;
9  import com.amazonaws.services.polly.model.VoiceId;
10
11 import java.io.File;
12 import java.io.FileOutputStream;
13 import java.io.InputStream;
14
15 public class SynthesizeSpeechMarksSample {
16     AmazonPolly client = AmazonPollyClientBuilder.defaultClient();
17
18     public void synthesizeSpeechMarks() {
19         String outputFileName = "/tmp/speechMarks.json";
20
21         SynthesizeSpeechRequest synthesizeSpeechRequest = new SynthesizeSpeechRequest()
22                 .withOutputFormat(OutputFormat.Json)
23                 .withSpeechMarkTypes(SpeechMarkType.Viseme, SpeechMarkType.Word)
24                 .withVoiceId(VoiceId.Joanna)
25                 .withText("This is a sample text to be synthesized.");
26
27         try (FileOutputStream outputStream = new FileOutputStream(new File(outputFileName))) {
28             SynthesizeSpeechResult synthesizeSpeechResult = client.synthesizeSpeech(
                    synthesizeSpeechRequest);
29             byte[] buffer = new byte[2 * 1024];
30             int readBytes;
31
32             try (InputStream in = synthesizeSpeechResult.getAudioStream()){
33                 while ((readBytes = in.read(buffer)) > 0) {
34                     outputStream.write(buffer, 0, readBytes);
35                 }
36             }
37         } catch (Exception e) {
38             System.err.println("Exception caught: " + e);
39         }
40     }
41 }
```

Speech Mark Types

You request speech marks in the AWS CLI using the `speech-mark-types` option for the `synthesize-speech` command. You specify the metadata elements that you want to return from your input text. You can request as many as four types of metada but you must specify at least one per request. No audio output is generated with the request.

```
1 --speech-mark-types='["sentence", "word", "viseme", "ssml"]'
```

Amazon Polly generates speech marks using the following elements:

- **sentence** – Indicates a sentence element in the input text.

- **word** – Indicates a word element in the text.

- **viseme** – Describes the face and mouth movements corresponding to each phoneme being spoken. For more information, see Visemes and Amazon Polly.

- **ssml** – Describes a element from the SSML input text. For more information, see Using SSML.

Visemes and Amazon Polly

A *viseme* represents the position of the face and mouth when saying a word. It is the visual equivalent of a phoneme, which is the basic acoustic unit from which a word is formed. Visemes are the basic visual building blocks of speech.

Each language has a set of viseme that correspond to their specific phonemes.. In a language, each phoneme has a corresponding viseme that represents the shape that the mouth makes when forming the sound. However, not all visemes can be mapped to a particular phoneme because numerous phonemes appear the same when spoken, even though they sound different. For example, in English, the words "pet" and "bet" are acoustically different. However, when observed visually (without sound), they look exactly the same.

The following chart lists the full set of International Phonetic Alphabet (IPA) phonemes and the Extended Speech Assessment Methods Phonetic Alphabet (X-SAMPA) symbols as well as their corresponding visemes for American English language voices.

IPA	X-SAMPA	Description	Example	Viseme
Consonants				
b	b	Voiced bilabial plosive	bed	p
d	d	Voiced alveolar plosive	dig	t
d	dZ	Voiced postalveolar affricate	jump	S
ð	D	Voiced dental fricative	then	T
f	f	Voiceless labiodental fricative	five	f
g	g	Voiced velar plosive	game	k
h	h	Voiceless glottal fricative	house	k
j	j	Palatal approximant	yes	i
k	k	Voiceless velar plosive	cat	k
l	l	Alveolar lateral approximant	lay	t
m	m	Bilabial nasal	mouse	p
n	n	Alveolar nasal	nap	t
ŋ	N	Velar nasal	thing	k
p	p	Voiceless bilabial plosive	speak	p
	r\	Alveolar approximant	red	r
s	s	Voiceless alveolar fricative	seem	s
	S	Voiceless postalveolar fricative	ship	S
t	t	Voiceless alveolar plosive	trap	t
t	tS	Voiceless postalveolar affricate	chart	S
Θ	T	Voiceless dental fricative	thin	T

27

IPA	X-SAMPA	Description	Example	Viseme
v	v	Voiced labiodental fricative	vest	f
w	w	Labial-velar approximant	west	u
z	z	Voiced alveolar fricative	zero	s
	Z	Voiced postalveolar fricative	vision	S
Vowels				
ə	@	Mid central vowel	arena	@
	@'	Mid central r-colored vowel	reader	@
æ	{	Near open-front unrounded vowel	trap	a
a	aI	Diphthong	price	a
a	aU	Diphthong	mouth	a
	A	Long open-back unrounded vowel	father	a
e	eI	Diphthong	face	e
	3'	Open mid-central unrounded r-colored vowel	nurse	E
	E	Open mid-front unrounded vowel	dress	E
i:	i	Long close front unrounded vowel	fleece	i
	I	Near-close near-front unrounded vowel	kit	i
o	oU	Diphthong	goat	o
	O	Long open mid-back rounded vowel	thought	O
	OI	Diphthong	choice	O
u	u	Long close-back rounded vowel	goose	u
	U	Near-close near-back rounded vowel	foot	u
	V	Open-mid-back unrounded vowel	strut	E

For all available languages, see Phoneme/Viseme Tables for Supported Languages.

Using Speech Marks

Requesting Speech Marks

To request speech marks for input text, use the `synthesize-speech` command. Besides the input text, the following elements are required to return this metadata:

- `output-format`

  Amazon Polly supports only the JSON format when returning speech marks.

  ```
  1 --output-format json
  ```

  If you use an unsupported output format, Amazon Polly throws an exception.

- `voice-id`

  To ensure that the metadata matches the associated audio stream, specify the same voice that is used to generate the synthesized speech audio stream. The available voices don't have identical speech rates. If you use a voice other than the one used to generate the speech, the metadata will not match the audio stream.

  ```
  1 --voice-id Joanna
  ```

- `speech-mark-types`

  Specify the type or types of speech marks you want. You can request any or all of the speech mark types, but must specify at least one type.

  ```
  1 --speech-mark-types='["sentence", "word", "viseme", "ssml"]'
  ```

- `text-type`

  Plain text is the default input text for Amazon Polly, so you must use `text-type ssml` if you want to return SSML speech marks.

- `outfile`

  Specify the output file to which the metadata is written.

  ```
  1 MaryLamb.txt
  ```

The following AWS CLI example is formatted for Unix, Linux, and macOS. For Windows, replace the backslash (\) Unix continuation character at the end of each line with a caret (^) and use full quotation marks (") around the input text with single quotes (') for interior tags.

```
1 aws polly synthesize-speech \
2   --output-format json \
3   --voice-id Voice ID \
4   --text 'Input text' \
5   --speech-mark-types='["sentence", "word", "viseme"]' \
6   outfile
```

Speech Mark Output

Amazon Polly returns speech mark objects in a line-delimited JSON stream. A speech mark object contains the following fields:

- **time** – the timestamp in milliseconds from the beginning of the corresponding audio stream

- **type** – the type of speech mark (sentence, word, viseme, or ssml).

- **start** – the offset in bytes of the start of the object in the input text (not including viseme marks)

- **end** – the offset in bytes of the object's end in the input text (not including viseme marks)

- **value** – this varies depending on the type of speech mark

- **SSML**: SSML tag

- **viseme**: the viseme name

- **word** or **sentence**: a substring of the input text, as delimited by the start and end fields

For example, Amazon Polly generates the following `word` speech mark object from the text "Mary had a little lamb":

```
1 {"time":373,"type":"word","start":5,"end":8,"value":"had"}
```

The described word ("had") begins 373 milliseconds after the audio stream begins, and starts at byte 5 and ends at byte 8 of the input text.

Note

This metadata is for the `Joanna` voice-id. If you use another voice with the same input text, the metadata might differ.

Speech Mark Examples

The following examples of speech mark requests show how to make common requests and the output that they generate.

Example 1: Speech Marks Without SSML

The following example shows you what requested metadata looks like on your screen for the simple sentence: "Mary had a little lamb." For simplicity, we don't include SSML speech marks in this example.

The following AWS CLI example is formatted for Unix, Linux, and macOS. For Windows, replace the backslash (\) Unix continuation character at the end of each line with a caret (^) and use full quotation marks (") around the input text with single quotes (') for interior tags.

```
1 aws polly synthesize-speech \
2   --output-format json \
3   --voice-id Joanna \
4   --text 'Mary had a little lamb.' \
5   --speech-mark-types='["viseme", "word", "sentence"]' \
6   MaryLamb.txt
```

When you make this request, Amazon Polly returns the following in the .txt file:

```
1 {"time":0,"type":"sentence","start":0,"end":23,"value":"Mary had a little lamb."}
2 {"time":6,"type":"word","start":0,"end":4,"value":"Mary"}
3 {"time":6,"type":"viseme","value":"p"}
4 {"time":73,"type":"viseme","value":"E"}
5 {"time":180,"type":"viseme","value":"r"}
6 {"time":292,"type":"viseme","value":"i"}
7 {"time":373,"type":"word","start":5,"end":8,"value":"had"}
8 {"time":373,"type":"viseme","value":"k"}
9 {"time":460,"type":"viseme","value":"a"}
10 {"time":521,"type":"viseme","value":"t"}
11 {"time":604,"type":"word","start":9,"end":10,"value":"a"}
12 {"time":604,"type":"viseme","value":"@"}
13 {"time":643,"type":"word","start":11,"end":17,"value":"little"}
14 {"time":643,"type":"viseme","value":"t"}
15 {"time":739,"type":"viseme","value":"i"}
16 {"time":769,"type":"viseme","value":"t"}
17 {"time":799,"type":"viseme","value":"t"}
18 {"time":882,"type":"word","start":18,"end":22,"value":"lamb"}
19 {"time":882,"type":"viseme","value":"t"}
20 {"time":964,"type":"viseme","value":"a"}
21 {"time":1082,"type":"viseme","value":"p"}
```

In this output, each part of the text is broken out in terms of speech marks:

- The sentence "Mary had a little lamb."

- Each word in the text: "Mary", "had", "a", "little", and "lamb."

- The viseme for each sound in the corresponding audio stream: "p", "E", "r", "i", and so on. For more information on visemes see Visemes and Amazon Polly.

Example 2: Speech Marks with SSML

The process of generating speech marks from SSML-enhanced text is similar to the process when SSML is not present. Use the `synthesize-speech` command, and specify the SSML-enhanced text and the type of speech marks that you want, as shown in the following example. To make the example easier to read, we do not include viseme speech marks, but these could be included as well.

The following AWS CLI example is formatted for Unix, Linux, and macOS. For Windows, replace the backslash (\) Unix continuation character at the end of each line with a caret (^) and use full quotation marks (") around the input text with single quotes (') for interior tags.

```
1 aws polly synthesize-speech \
2   --output-format json \
3   --voice-id Joanna \
4   --text-type ssml \
5   --text '<speak><prosody volume="+20dB">Mary had <break time="300ms"/>a little <mark name="
        animal"/>lamb</prosody></speak>' \
6   --speech-mark-types='["sentence", "word", "ssml"]' \
7   output.txt
```

When you make this request, Amazon Polly returns the following in the .txt file:

```
1 {"time":0,"type":"sentence","start":31,"end":95,"value":"Mary had <break time=\"300ms\"\/>a
        little <mark name=\"animal\"\/>lamb"}
2 {"time":6,"type":"word","start":31,"end":35,"value":"Mary"}
3 {"time":325,"type":"word","start":36,"end":39,"value":"had"}
4 {"time":897,"type":"word","start":40,"end":61,"value":"<break time=\"300ms\"\/>"}
5 {"time":1291,"type":"word","start":61,"end":62,"value":"a"}
6 {"time":1373,"type":"word","start":63,"end":69,"value":"little"}
7 {"time":1635,"type":"ssml","start":70,"end":91,"value":"animal"}
8 {"time":1635,"type":"word","start":91,"end":95,"value":"lamb"}
```

Requesting Speech Marks Using the Amazon Polly Console

You can use the console to request speech marks from Amazon Polly. You can then view the metadata or save it to a file.

To generate speech marks from the Console

1. Sign in to the AWS Management Console and open the Amazon Polly console at https://console.aws. amazon.com/polly/.

2. Choose the **Text-to-Speech** tab.

3. Continue using the **Plain Text** tab or choose the **SSML** tab.

4. Type or paste your text into the input box.

5. For **Language and region**, choose the language for your text.

6. For **Voice**, choose the voice you want to use for the text.

7. To change text pronunciation, choose **Customize Pronunciation**, and for **Apply Lexicon** choose the desired lexicon.

8. To verify that the speech is in its final form, choose **Listen to speech**.

9. Choose **Change File Format. Note**
   Downloading MP3, OGG, or PCM formats will not generate speech marks.

10. For **File Format**, choose **Speech Marks**.

11. For **Speech Mark Types**, choose the types of speech marks to generate. The option to choose **SSML** metadata is only available on the **SSML** tab. For more information on using SSML with Amazon Polly see Using SSML.

12. Choose **Change**.

13. Choose **Download Speech Marks**.

Phoneme/Viseme Tables for Supported Languages

This section provides phoneme/viseme tables for the languages supported by Amazon Polly.

- Danish (da-DK)
- Dutch (nl-NL)
- English, Australian (en-AU)
- English, Indian (en-IN)
- English, British (en-GB)
- English, American (en-US)
- English, Welsh (en-GB-WSL)
- French (fr-FR)
- French, Canadian (fr-CA)
- German (de-DE)
- Icelandic (is-IS)
- Italian (it-IT)
- Japanese (ja-JP)
- Korean (ko-KR)
- Norwegian (nb-NO)
- Polish (pl-PL)
- Portuguese (pt-PT)
- Portuguese, Brazilian (pt-BR)
- Romanian (ro-RO)
- Russian (ru-RU)
- Spanish (es-ES)
- Spanish, US (es-US)
- Swedish (sv-SE)
- Turkish (tr-TR)
- Welsh (cy-GB)

Danish (da-DK)

The following table lists the International Phonetic Alphabet (IPA) phonemes, the Extended Speech Assessment Methods Phonetic Alphabet (X-SAMPA) symbols, and the corresponding visemes for the Danish voices that are supported by Amazon Polly.

Phoneme/Viseme Table

IPA	X-SAMPA	Description	Example	Viseme
Consonants				
b	b	voiced bilabial plosive	bat	p
d	d	voiced alveolar plosive	da	t
ð	D	voiced dental fricative	mad, thriller	T
f	f	voiceless labiodental fricative	fat	f
g	g	voiced velar plosive	gat	k
h	h	voiceless glottal fricative	hat	k
j	j	palatal approximant	jo	i
k	k	voiceless velar plosive	kat	k
l	l	alveolar lateral approximant	ladt	t
m	m	bilabial nasal	mat	p
n	n	alveolar nasal	nay	t
ŋ	N	velar nasal	lang	k
p	p	voiceless bilabial plosive	pande	p
r	r	alveolar trill	thriller, story	r
	R	voiced uvular fricative	rat	k
s	s	voiceless alveolar fricative	sat	s
t	t	voiceless alveolar plosive	tal	t
v	v	voiced labiodental fricative	vat	f
w	w	labial-velar approximant	hav, weekend	X
Vowels				
ø	2	close-mid front rounded vowel	øst	o
ø:	2:	long close-mid front rounded vowel	øse	o
	6	near-open central vowel	mor	a
œ	9	open-mid front rounded vowel	skøn, grønt	O

IPA	X-SAMPA	Description	Example	Viseme
œ:	9:	long open-mid front rounded vowel	høne, gøre	O
ə	@	mid central vowel	ane	@
æ	{:	long near-open front unrounded vowel	male	a
a	a	open front unrounded vowel	man	a
æ	{	near-open front unrounded vowel	adresse	a
	A	open back unrounded vowel	lak, tak	a
:	A:	long open back unrounded vowel	rase	a

Dutch (nl-NL)

The following table lists the International Phonetic Alphabet (IPA) phonemes, the Extended Speech Assessment Methods Phonetic Alphabet (X-SAMPA) symbols, and the corresponding visemes for the Dutch voices that are supported by Amazon Polly.

Phoneme/Viseme Table

IPA	X-SAMPA	Description	Example	Viseme
Consonants				
b	b	voiced bilabial plosive	bak	p
d	d	voiced alveolar plosive	dak	t
d	dZ	voiced postalveolar affricate	manager	S
f	f	voiceless labiodental fricative	fel	f
g	g	voiced velar plosive	goal	k
	G	voiced velar fricative	hoed	k
	h\	voiced glottal fricative	hand	k
j	j	palatal approximant	ja	i
k	k	voiceless velar plosive	kap	k
l	l	alveolar lateral approximant	land	t
m	m	bilabial nasal	met	p
n	n	alveolar nasal	net	t
ŋ	N	velar nasal	bang	k
p	p	voiceless bilabial plosive	pak	p
r	r	alveolar trill	rand	r
s	s	voiceless alveolar fricative	sein	s
	S	voiceless postalveolar fricative	show	S
t	t	voiceless alveolar plosive	tak	t
v	v	voiced labiodental fricative	vel	f
	v\	labiodental approximant	wit	f
x	x	voiceless velar fricative	toch	k
z	z	voiced alveolar fricative	ziin	s
	Z	voiced postalveolar fricative	bagage	S
Vowels				

IPA	X-SAMPA	Description	Example	Viseme
ø	2:	long close-mid front rounded vowel	n**eu**s	o
œy	9y	diphthong	b**ui**t	O
ə	@	mid central vowel	d**e**	@
a:	a:	long open front unrounded vowel	b**aa**d	a
:	A	open back unrounded vowel	b**a**d	a
e:	e:	long close-mid front unrounded vowel	b**ee**t	e
	3:	long open-mid central unrounded vowel	barri**è**re	E
	E	open-mid front unrounded vowel	b**e**d	E
i	Ei	diphthong	b**ee**t	E
i	i	close front unrounded vowel	v**ie**r	i
	I	near-close near-front unrounded vowel	p**i**t	i
o:	o:	long close-mid back rounded vowel	b**oo**t	o
	O	open-mid back rounded vowel	p**o**t	O
u	u	close back rounded vowel	h**oe**d	u
u	Vu	diphthong	f**ou**t	E
y	y:	long close front rounded vowel	f**uu**t	u
	Y	near-close near-front rounded vowel	h**u**t	u

English, Australian (en-AU)

The following table lists the International Phonetic Alphabet (IPA) phonemes, the Extended Speech Assessment Methods Phonetic Alphabet (X-SAMPA) symbols, and the corresponding visemes for the Australian English voices that are supported by Amazon Polly.

Phoneme/Viseme Table

IPA	X-SAMPA	Description	Example	Viseme
Consonants				
b	b	voiced bilabial plosive	bed	p
d	d	voiced alveolar plosive	dig	t
d	dZ	voiced postalveolar affricate	jump	S
ð	D	voiced dental fricative	then	T
f	f	voiceless labiodental fricative	five	f
g	g	voiced velar plosive	game	k
h	h	voiceless glottal fricative	house	k
j	j	palatal approximant	yes	i
k	k	voiceless velar plosive	cat	k
l	l	alveolar lateral approximant	lay	t
l	l=	syllabic alveolar lateral approximant	battle	t
m	m	bilabial nasal	mouse	p
m	m=	syllabic bilabial nasal	anthem	p
n	n	alveolar nasal	nap	t
n	n=	syllabic alveolar nasal	nap	t
ŋ	N	velar nasal	thing	k
p	p	voiceless bilabial plosive	pin	p
	r\	alveolar approximant	red	r
s	s	voiceless alveolar fricative	seem	s
	S	voiceless postalveolar fricative	ship	S
t	t	voiceless alveolar plosive	task	t
t	tS	voiceless postalveolar affricate	chart	S
Θ	T	voiceless dental fricative	thin	T

39

IPA	X-SAMPA	Description	Example	Viseme
v	v	voiced labiodental fricative	**v**est	f
w	w	labial-velar approximant	**w**est	u
z	z	voiced alveolar fricative	**z**ero	s
	Z	voiced postalveolar fricative	vi**s**ion	S
Vowels				
ə	@	mid central vowel	**a**rena	@
ə	@U	diphthong	g**oa**t	@
æ	{	near open-front unrounded vowel	tr**a**p	a
a	aI	diphthong	pr**i**ce	a
a	aU	diphthong	m**ou**th	a
	A:	long open-back unrounded vowel	f**a**ther	a
e	eI	diphthong	f**a**ce	e
	3:	long open mid-central unrounded vowel	n**ur**se	E
	E	open mid-front unrounded vowel	dr**e**ss	E
ə	E@	diphthong	squ**are**	E
i:	i	long close front unrounded vowel	fl**ee**ce	i
	I	near-close near-front unrounded vowel	k**i**t	i
ə	I@	diphthong	**near**	i
	OI	long open-mid back rounded vowel	th**ou**ght	O
	OI	Diphthong	ch**oi**ce	O
	Q	open back rounded vowel	l**o**t	O
u:	u:	long close-back rounded vowel	g**oo**se	u
	U	near-close near-back rounded vowel	f**oo**t	u
ə	U@	diphthong	c**ure**	u
	V	Open-mid-back unrounded vowel	str**u**t	E

English, Indian (en-IN)

The following table lists the International Phonetic Alphabet (IPA) phonemes, the Extended Speech Assessment Methods Phonetic Alphabet (X-SAMPA) symbols, and the corresponding visemes for the Indian English voice supported by Amazon Polly.

Phoneme/Viseme Table

IPA	X-SAMPA	Description	Example	Viseme
Consonants				
b	b	voiced bilabial plosive	bed	p
d	d	voiced alveolar plosive	dig	t
d	dZ	voiced postalveolar affricate	jump	S
ð	D	voiced dental fricative	then	T
f	f	voiceless labiodental fricative	five	f
g	g	voiced velar plosive	game	k
h	h	voiceless glottal fricative	house	k
j	j	palatal approximant	yes	i
k	k	voiceless velar plosive	cat	k
l	l	alveolar lateral approximant	lay	t
l	l=	syllabic alveolar lateral approximant	battle	t
m	m	bilabial nasal	mouse	p
m	m=	syllabic bilabial nasal	anthem	p
n	n	alveolar nasal	nap	t
n	n=	syllabic alveolar nasal	nap	t
ŋ	N	velar nasal	thing	k
p	p	voiceless bilabial plosive	pin	p
	r\	alveolar approximant	red	r
s	s	voiceless alveolar fricative	seem	s
	S	voiceless postalveolar fricative	ship	S
t	t	voiceless alveolar plosive	task	t
t	tS	voiceless postalveolar affricate	chart	S
Θ	T	voiceless dental fricative	thin	T

41

IPA	X-SAMPA	Description	Example	Viseme
v	v	voiced labiodental fricative	**v**est	f
w	w	labial-velar approximant	**w**est	u
z	z	voiced alveolar fricative	**z**ero	s
	Z	voiced postalveolar fricative	vi**si**on	S
Vowels				
ə	@	mid central vowel	**a**rena	@
ə	@U	diphthong	g**oa**t	@
æ	{	near open-front unrounded vowel	tr**a**p	a
a	aI	diphthong	pr**i**ce	a
a	aU	diphthong	m**ou**th	a
	A:	long open-back unrounded vowel	f**a**ther	a
e	eI	diphthong	f**a**ce	e
	3:	long open mid-central unrounded vowel	n**ur**se	E
	E	open mid-front unrounded vowel	dr**e**ss	E
ə	E@	diphthong	sq**ua**re	E
i:	i	long close front unrounded vowel	fl**ee**ce	i
	I	near-close near-front unrounded vowel	k**i**t	i
ə	I@	diphthong	n**ear**	i
	OI	long open-mid back rounded vowel	th**ou**ght	O
	OI	Diphthong	ch**oi**ce	O
	Q	open back rounded vowel	l**o**t	O
u:	u:	long close-back rounded vowel	g**oo**se	u
	U	near-close near-back rounded vowel	f**oo**t	u
ə	U@	diphthong	c**u**re	u
	V	Open-mid-back unrounded vowel	str**u**t	E

English, British (en-GB)

The following table lists the International Phonetic Alphabet (IPA) phonemes, the Extended Speech Assessment Methods Phonetic Alphabet (X-SAMPA) symbols, and the corresponding visemes for the British English voices that are supported by Amazon Polly.

Phoneme/Viseme Table

IPA	X-SAMPA	Description	Example	Viseme
Consonants				
b	b	voiced bilabial plosive	bed	p
d	d	voiced alveolar plosive	dig	t
d	dZ	voiced postalveolar affricate	jump	S
ð	D	voiced dental fricative	then	T
f	f	voiceless labiodental fricative	five	f
g	g	voiced velar plosive	game	k
h	h	voiceless glottal fricative	house	k
j	j	palatal approximant	yes	i
k	k	voiceless velar plosive	cat	k
l	l	alveolar lateral approximant	lay	t
l	l=	syllabic alveolar lateral approximant	battle	t
m	m	bilabial nasal	mouse	p
m	m=	syllabic bilabial nasal	anthem	p
n	n	alveolar nasal	nap	t
n	n=	syllabic alveolar nasal	button	t
ŋ	N	velar nasal	thing	k
p	p	voiceless bilabial plosive	pin	p
	r\	alveolar approximant	red	r
s	s	voiceless alveolar fricative	seem	s
	S	voiceless postalveolar fricative	ship	S
t	t	voiceless alveolar plosive	task	t
t	tS	voiceless postalveolar affricate	chart	S
Θ	T	voiceless dental fricative	thin	T

43

IPA	X-SAMPA	Description	Example	Viseme
v	v	voiced labiodental fricative	**v**est	f
w	w	labial-velar approximant	**w**est	u
z	z	voiced alveolar fricative	**z**ero	s
	Z	voiced postalveolar fricative	vi**s**ion	S
Vowels				
ə	@	mid central vowel	**a**ren**a**	@
ə	@U	diphthong	g**oa**t	@
æ	{	near open-front unrounded vowel	tr**a**p	a
a	aI	diphthong	pr**i**ce	a
a	aU	diphthong	m**ou**th	a
	A:	long open-back unrounded vowel	f**a**ther	a
e	eI	diphthong	f**a**ce	e
	3:	long open mid-central unrounded vowel	n**ur**se	E
	E	open mid-front unrounded vowel	dr**e**ss	E
ə	E@	diphthong	sq**ua**re	E
i:	i	long close front unrounded vowel	fl**ee**ce	i
	I	near-close near-front unrounded vowel	k**i**t	i
ə	I@	diphthong	**near**	i
	O:	long open-mid back rounded vowel	th**ough**t	O
	OI	Diphthong	ch**oi**ce	O
	Q	open back rounded vowel	l**o**t	O
u:	u:	long close-back rounded vowel	g**oo**se	u
	U	near-close near-back rounded vowel	f**oo**t	u
ə	U@	diphthong	c**u**re	u
	V	Open-mid-back unrounded vowel	str**u**t	E

English, American (en-US)

The following table lists the International Phonetic Alphabet (IPA) phonemes, the Extended Speech Assessment Methods Phonetic Alphabet (X-SAMPA) symbols, and the corresponding visemes for the American English voices that are supported by Amazon Polly.

Phoneme/Viseme Table

IPA	X-SAMPA	Description	Example	Viseme
Consonants				
b	b	voiced bilabial plosive	bed	p
d	d	voiced alveolar plosive	dig	t
d	dZ	voiced postalveolar affricate	jump	S
ð	D	voiced dental fricative	then	T
f	f	voiceless labiodental fricative	five	f
g	g	voiced velar plosive	game	k
h	h	voiceless glottal fricative	house	k
j	j	palatal approximant	yes	i
k	k	voiceless velar plosive	cat	k
l	l	alveolar lateral approximant	lay	t
m	m	bilabial nasal	mouse	p
n	n	alveolar nasal	nap	t
ŋ	N	velar nasal	thing	k
p	p	voiceless bilabial plosive	speak	p
	r\	alveolar approximant	red	r
s	s	voiceless alveolar fricative	seem	s
	S	voiceless postalveolar fricative	ship	S
t	t	voiceless alveolar plosive	trap	t
t	tS	voiceless postalveolar affricate	chart	S
Θ	T	voiceless dental fricative	thin	T
v	v	voiced labiodental fricative	vest	f
w	w	labial-velar approximant	west	u
z	z	voiced alveolar fricative	zero	s

IPA	X-SAMPA	Description	Example	Viseme
	Z	voiced postalveolar fricative	vision	S
Vowels				
ə	@	mid-central vowel	arena	@
	@'	mid-central r-colored vowel	reader	@
æ	{	near open-front unrounded vowel	trap	a
a	aI	diphthong	price	a
a	aU	diphthong	mouth	a
	A	long open-back unrounded vowel	father	a
e	eI	diphthong	face	e
	3'	open mid-central unrounded r-colored vowel	nurse	E
	E	open mid-front unrounded vowel	dress	E
i:	i	long close front unrounded vowel	fleece	i
	I	near-close near-front unrounded vowel	kit	i
o	oU	diphthong	goat	o
	O	long open mid-back rounded vowel	thought	O
	OI	diphthong	choice	O
u	u	long close-back rounded vowel	goose	u
	U	near-close near-back rounded vowel	foot	u
	V	open-mid-back unrounded vowel	strut	E

English, Welsh (en-GB-WSL)

The following table lists the International Phonetic Alphabet (IPA) phonemes, the Extended Speech Assessment Methods Phonetic Alphabet (X-SAMPA) symbols, and the corresponding visemes for the Welsh English voice supported by Amazon Polly.

Phoneme/Viseme Table

IPA	X-SAMPA	Description	Example	Viseme
Consonants				
b	b	voiced bilabial plosive	bed	p
d	d	voiced alveolar plosive	dig	t
d	dZ	voiced postalveolar affricate	jump	S
ð	D	voiced dental fricative	then	T
f	f	voiceless labiodental fricative	five	f
g	g	voiced velar plosive	game	k
h	h	voiceless glottal fricative	house	k
j	j	palatal approximant	yes	i
k	k	voiceless velar plosive	cat	k
l	l	alveolar lateral approximant	lay	t
l	l=	syllabic alveolar lateral approximant	battle	t
m	m	bilabial nasal	mouse	p
m	m=	syllabic bilabial nasal	anthem	p
n	n	alveolar nasal	nap	t
n	n=	syllabic alveolar nasal	nap	t
ŋ	N	velar nasal	thing	k
p	p	voiceless bilabial plosive	pin	p
	r\	alveolar approximant	red	r
s	s	voiceless alveolar fricative	seem	s
	S	voiceless postalveolar fricative	ship	S
t	t	voiceless alveolar plosive	task	t
t	tS	voiceless postalveolar affricate	chart	S
Θ	T	voiceless dental fricative	thin	T

47

IPA	X-SAMPA	Description	Example	Viseme
v	v	voiced labiodental fricative	**v**est	f
w	w	labial-velar approximant	**w**est	u
z	z	voiced alveolar fricative	**z**ero	s
Z	Z	voiced postalveolar fricative	vi**s**ion	S
Vowels				
ə	@	mid central vowel	**a**rena	@
ə	@U	diphthong	g**oa**t	@
æ	{	near open-front unrounded vowel	tr**a**p	a
a	aI	diphthong	pr**i**ce	a
a	aU	diphthong	m**ou**th	a
	A:	long open-back unrounded vowel	f**a**ther	a
e	eI	diphthong	f**a**ce	e
	3:	long open mid-central unrounded vowel	n**ur**se	E
	E	open mid-front unrounded vowel	dr**e**ss	E
ə	E@	diphthong	squ**are**	E
i:	i	long close front unrounded vowel	fl**ee**ce	i
	I	near-close near-front unrounded vowel	k**i**t	i
ə	I@	diphthong	n**ear**	i
	OI	long open-mid back rounded vowel	th**ou**ght	O
	OI	Diphthong	ch**oi**ce	O
	Q	open back rounded vowel	l**o**t	O
u:	u:	long close-back rounded vowel	g**oo**se	u
	U	near-close near-back rounded vowel	f**oo**t	u
ə	U@	diphthong	c**ure**	u
	V	Open-mid-back unrounded vowel	str**u**t	E

French (fr-FR)

The following table lists the International Phonetic Alphabet (IPA) phonemes, the Extended Speech Assessment Methods Phonetic Alphabet (X-SAMPA) symbols, and the corresponding visemes for the French voices that are supported by Amazon Polly.

Phoneme/Viseme Table

IPA	X-SAMPA	Description	Example	Viseme
Consonants				
b	b	voiced bilabial plosive	boire	p
d	d	voiced alveolar plosive	madame	t
f	f	voiceless labiodental fricative	femme	f
g	g	voiced velar plosive	grand	k
	H	labial-palatal approximant	bruit	u
j	j	palatal approximant	meilleur	i
k	k	voiceless velar plosive	quatre	k
l	l	alveolar lateral approximant	malade	t
m	m	bilabial nasal	maison	p
n	n	alveolar nasal	astronome	t
	J	palatal nasal	baigner	J
ŋ	N	velar nasal	parking	k
p	p	voiceless bilabial plosive	pomme	p
	R\	uvular trill	amoureux	k
s	s	voiceless alveolar fricative	santé	s
	S	voiceless postalveolar fricative	chat	S
t	t	voiceless alveolar plosive	téléphone	t
v	v	voiced labiodental fricative	vrai	f
w	w	labial-velar approximant	soir	u
z	z	voiced alveolar fricative	raison	s
	Z	voiced postalveolar fricative	aubergine	S
Vowels				
ø	2	close-mid front rounded vowel	deux	o
œ	9	open-mid front rounded vowel	neuf	O

IPA	X-SAMPA	Description	Example	Viseme
œ̃	9~	nasal open-mid front rounded vowel	br**un**	O
ə	@	mid central vowel	j**e**	@
a	a	open front unrounded vowel	t**a**ble	a
~	A~	nasal open back unrounded vowel	cam**em**bert	a
e	e	close-mid front unrounded vowel	march**é**	e
	E	open-mid front unrounded vowel	n**ei**ge	E
~	E~	nasal open-mid front unrounded vowel	sap**in**	E
i	i	close front unrounded vowel	m**i**lle	i
o	o	close-mid back rounded vowel	h**o**mme	o
	O	open-mid back rounded vowel	h**ô**pital	O
~	O~	nasal open-mid back rounded vowel	b**on**	O
u	u	close back rounded vowel	s**ou**s	u
y	y	close front rounded vowel	d**ur**	u

French, Canadian (fr-CA)

The following table lists the International Phonetic Alphabet (IPA) phonemes, the Extended Speech Assessment Methods Phonetic Alphabet (X-SAMPA) symbols, and the corresponding visemes for the French Canadian voice supported by Amazon Polly.

Phoneme/Viseme Table

IPA	X-SAMPA	Description	Example	Viseme
Consonants				
b	b	voiced bilabial plosive	boire	p
d	d	voiced alveolar plosive	madame	t
f	f	voiceless labiodental fricative	femme	f
g	g	voiced velar plosive	grand	k
	H	labial-palatal approximant	bruit	u
j	j	palatal approximant	meilleur	i
k	k	voiceless velar plosive	quatre	k
l	l	alveolar lateral approximant	malade	t
m	m	bilabial nasal	maison	p
n	n	alveolar nasal	astronome	t
	J	palatal nasal	baigner	J
ŋ	N	velar nasal	parking	k
p	p	voiceless bilabial plosive	pomme	p
	R\	uvular trill	amoureux	k
s	s	voiceless alveolar fricative	santé	s
	S	voiceless postalveolar fricative	chat	S
t	t	voiceless alveolar plosive	téléphone	t
v	v	voiced labiodental fricative	vrai	f
w	w	labial-velar approximant	soir	u
z	z	voiced alveolar fricative	raison	s
	Z	voiced postalveolar fricative	aubergine	S
Vowels				
ø	2	close-mid front rounded vowel	deux	o
œ	9	open-mid front rounded vowel	neuf	O

IPA	X-SAMPA	Description	Example	Viseme
œ̃	9~	nasal open-mid front rounded vowel	br**un**	O
ə	@	mid central vowel	**je**	@
a	a	open front unrounded vowel	**ta**ble	a
~	A~	nasal open back unrounded vowel	came**m**bert	a
e	e	close-mid front unrounded vowel	march**é**	e
	E	open-mid front unrounded vowel	**ne**ige	E
~	E~	nasal open-mid front unrounded vowel	sap**in**	E
i	i	close front unrounded vowel	m**i**lle	i
o	o	close-mid back rounded vowel	h**o**mme	o
	O	open-mid back rounded vowel	h**ô**pital	O
~	O~	nasal open-mid back rounded vowel	b**on**	O
u	u	close back rounded vowel	s**ou**s	u
y	y	close front rounded vowel	d**u**r	u

German (de-DE)

The following table lists the International Phonetic Alphabet (IPA) phonemes, the Extended Speech Assessment Methods Phonetic Alphabet (X-SAMPA) symbols, and the corresponding visemes for the German voices that are supported by Amazon Polly.

Phoneme/Viseme Table

IPA	X-SAMPA	Description	Example	Viseme
Consonants				
	?	glottal stop		
b	b	voiced bilabial plosive	**B**ier	p
d	d	voiced alveolar plosive	**D**ach	t
ç	C	voiceless palatal fricative	i**ch**	k
d	dZ	voiced postalveolar affricate	**Dsch**ungel	S
f	f	Voiceless labiodental fricative	**V**ogel	f
g	g	Voiced velar plosive	**G**abel	k
h	h	Voiceless glottal fricative	**H**aus	k
j	j	Voiceless glottal fricative	**j**emand	i
k	k	Voiceless velar plosive	**K**leid	k
l	l	Alveolar lateral approximant	**L**och	t
m	m	Bilabial nasal	**M**ilch	p
n	n	Alveolar nasal	**N**atur	t
ŋ	N	Velar nasal	kli**ng**en	k
p	p	Voiceless bilabial plosive	**P**ark	p
pf	pf	Voiceless labiodental affricate	**Apf**el	
	R	Uvular trill	**R**egen	
s	s	voiceless alveolar fricative	Me**ss**er	s
	S	Voiceless postalveolar fricative	Fi**sch**er	S
t	t	Voiceless alveolar plosive	**T**opf	T
ts	Ts	Voiceless alveolar affricate	**Z**ahl	
t	tS	Voiceless postalveolar affricate	deu**tsch**	S
v	v	Voiced labiodental fricative	**W**asser	f
x	x	Voiceless velar fricative	ko**ch**en	k

IPA	X-SAMPA	Description	Example	Viseme
z	z	Voiced alveolar fricative	See	s
	Z	Voiced postalveolar fricative	Orange	S
Vowels				
ø	2:	long close-mid front rounded vowel	böse	o
	6	near-open central vowel	besser	a
^	6_^	non-syllabic near-open central vowel	Klar	a
œ	9	open-mid front rounded vowel	können	O
ə	@	mid central vowel	Rede	@
a	a	open front unrounded vowel	Salz	a
a:	a:	long open front unrounded vowel	Sahne	a
a	aI	diphthong	nein	a
a	aU	diphthong	Augen	a
~	A~	nasal open back unrounded vowel	Restaurant	a
e:	e:	long close-mid front unrounded vowel	Rede	e
	E	open-mid front unrounded vowel	Keller	E
~	E~	nasal open-mid front unrounded vowel	Terrain	E
i:	i:	long close front unrounded vowel	Lied	i
	I	near-close near-front unrounded vowel	bitte	i
o:	o:	long close-mid back rounded vowel	Kohl	o
	O	open-mid back rounded vowel	Koffer	O
~	O~	nasal open-mid back rounded vowel	Annonce	O
	OY	diphthong	neu	O
u:	u:	long close back rounded vowel	Bruder	u
	U	near-close near-back rounded vowel	Wunder	u
y:	y:	long close front rounded vowel	kühl	u

IPA	X-SAMPA	Description	Example	Viseme
	Y	near-close near-front rounded vowel	K**ü**che	u

Icelandic (is-IS)

The following table lists the International Phonetic Alphabet (IPA) phonemes, the Extended Speech Assessment Methods Phonetic Alphabet (X-SAMPA) symbols, and the corresponding visemes for the Icelandic voices that are supported by Amazon Polly.

Phoneme/Viseme Table

IPA	X-SAMPA	Description	Example	Viseme
Consonants				
b	b	voiced bilabial plosive	grasbakkanum	0
c	c	voiceless palatal plosive	pakkin	k
c	c_h	aspirated voiceless palatal plosive	anarkistai	k
ç	C	voiceless palatal fricative	héðan	k
d	d	voiced alveolar plosive	bóndi	t
ð	D	voiced dental fricative	borð	T
f	f	voiceless labiodental fricative	duft	f
g	g	voiced velar plosive	holgóma	k
	G	voiced velar fricative	hugur	k
h	h	voiceless glottal fricative	heili	k
j	j	palatal approximant	jökull	i
k	k_h	aspirated voiceless velar plosive	ósköpunum	k
l	l	alveolar lateral approximant	gólf	t
l	l_0	voiceless alveolar lateral approximant	fólk	t
m	m	bilabial nasal	september	p
m	m_0	voiceless bilabial nasal	kompa	p
n	n	alveolar nasal	númer	t
n	n_0	voiceless alveolar nasal	pöntun	t
	J	palatal nasal	pælingar	J
ŋ	N	velar nasal	söngvarann	k
ŋ̊	N_0	voiceless velar nasal	frænka	k
p	p_h	aspirated voiceless bilabial plosive	afplánun	p
r	r	alveolar trill	afskrifta	r

IPA	X-SAMPA	Description	Example	Viseme
r	r_0	voiceless alveolar trill	andvörpum	r
s	s	voiceless alveolar fricative	baðhús	s
t	t_h	aspirated voiceless alveolar plosive	tanki	t
	T	voiceless dental fricative	þeldökki	T
v	v	voiced labiodental fricative	silfur	f
w	w	labial-velar approximant		u
x	x	voiceless velar fricative	samfélags	k
Vowels				
œ	9	open-mid front rounded vowel	þröskuldinum	O
œ	9:	long open-mid front rounded vowel	tvö	O
a	a	open front unrounded vowel	nefna	a
a:	a:	long open front unrounded vowel	fara	a
au	au	diphthong	átta	a
au:	au:	diphthong	átján	a
	E	open-mid front unrounded vowel	kennari	E
:	E:	long open-mid front unrounded vowel	dreka	E
i	i	close front unrounded vowel	Gúlíver	i
i:	i:	long close front unrounded vowel	þrír	i
	I	near-close near-front unrounded vowel	samspil	i
:	I:	long near-close near-front unrounded vowel	stig	i
	O	open-mid back rounded vowel	regndropar	O
:	O:	long open-mid back rounded vowel	ullarbolur	O
u	Ou	diphthong	tólf	O
u:	Ou:	diphthong	fjórir	O
u	u	close back rounded vowel	stúlkan	u
u:	u:	long close back rounded vowel	frú	u

IPA	X-SAMPA	Description	Example	Viseme
	Y	near-close near-front rounded vowel	tíu	u
:	Y	long near-close near-front rounded vowel	gruninn	u

Italian (it-IT)

The following table lists the International Phonetic Alphabet (IPA) phonemes, the Extended Speech Assessment Methods Phonetic Alphabet (X-SAMPA) symbols, and the corresponding visemes for the Italian voices that are supported by Amazon Polly.

Phoneme/Viseme Table

IPA	X-SAMPA	Description	Example	Viseme
Consonants				
b	b	voiced bilabial plosive	bacca	p
d	d	voiced alveolar plosive	dama	t
dz	dz	voiced alveolar affricate	zero	s
d	dZ	voiced postalveolar affricate	giro	S
f	f	voiceless labiodental fricative	famiglia	f
g	g	voiced velar plosive	gatto	k
h	h	voiceless glottal fricative	horror	k
j	j	palatal approximant	dieci	i
k	k	voiceless velar plosive	campo	k
l	l	alveolar lateral approximant	lido	t
	L	palatal lateral approximant	aglio	J
m	m	bilabial nasal	mille	p
n	n	alveolar nasal	nove	t
	J	palatal nasal	lasagne	J
p	p	voiceless bilabial plosive	pizza	p
r	r	alveolar trill	risata	r
s	s	voiceless alveolar fricative	sei	s
	S	voiceless postalveolar fricative	scienza	S
t	t	voiceless alveolar plosive	tavola	t
ts	ts	voiceless alveolar affricate	forza	s
t	tS	voiceless postalveolar affricate	cielo	S
v	v	voiced labiodental fricative	venti	f
w	w	labial-velar approximant	quattro	u
z	z	voiced alveolar fricative	bisogno	s

IPA	X-SAMPA	Description	Example	Viseme
	Z	voiced postalveolar fricative	bijou	S
Vowels				
a	a	open front unrounded vowel	arco	a
e	e	close-mid front unrounded vowel	tre	e
	E	open-mid front unrounded vowel	ettaro	E
i	i	close front unrounded vowel	impero	i
o	o	close-mid back rounded vowel	cento	o
	O	open-mid back rounded vowel	otto	O
u	u	close back rounded vowel	uno	u

Japanese (ja-JP)

The following table lists the International Phonetic Alphabet (IPA) phonemes, the Extended Speech Assessment Methods Phonetic Alphabet (X-SAMPA) symbols, and the corresponding visemes for the Japanese voice supported by Amazon Polly.

IPA	X-SAMPA	Description	Example	Viseme
Consonants				
	4	alveolar flap	, renshuu	t
	?	glottal stop	, atsu**'**	
b	b	voiced bilabial plosive	, buyou	p
	B	voiced bilabial fricative	, vinteeji	B
c	c	voiceless palatal plosive	, kikyou	k
ç	C	voiceless palatal fricative	, hito	k
d	d	voiced alveolar plosive	, dakuten	t
d	dz\	voiced alveolo-palatal affricate	, jun	J
	g	voiced velar plosive	, gohan	k
h	h	voiceless glottal fricative	, hon	k
j	j	palatal approximant	, yane	i
	J\	voiced palatal plosive	, gyougi	J
k	k	voiceless velar plosive	, kanji	k
	l\	alveolar lateral flap	, tsuri	r
j	l\j	alveolar lateral flap, palatal approximant	, ryuukou	r
m	m	bilabial nasal	, meshi	p
n	n	alveolar nasal	, neko	t
	J	palatal nasal	, nippon	J
	N\	uvular nasal	, kan	k
p	p	voiceless bilabial plosive	, pan	p
	p\	voiceless bilabial fricative	, huku	f
s	s	voiceless alveolar fricative	, sou	s
	s\	voiceless alveolo-palatal fricative	, shokan	J
t	t	voiceless alveolar plosive	, tegami	t
ts	ts	voiceless alveolar affricate	, tsuri	s

IPA	X-SAMPA	Description	Example	Viseme
t	ts\	voiceless alveolo-palatal affricate	, ki**chi**	J
w	w	labial-velar approximant	, den**wa**	u
z	z	voiced alveolar fricative	, **z**ashiki	s
Vowels				
ä	a:_"	long open central unrounded vowel	, h**aa**ri	a
ä	a_"	open central unrounded vowel	, k**a**n**a**	a
e	e:_o	long mid front unrounded vowel	, gakus**ei**	@
e	e_o	mid front unrounded vowel	, r**e**ki	@
i	i	close front unrounded vowel	, k**i**	i
i	i:	long close front unrounded vowel	, sh**ii**ka	i
	M	close back unrounded vowel	, **u**n	i
	M:	long close back unrounded vowel	, sh**uu**kyou	i
o	o:_o	long mid back rounded vowel	, k**oo**doku	o
o	o_o	mid back rounded vowel	, d**o**kusha	o

Korean (ko-KR)

The following table lists the International Phonetic Alphabet (IPA) phonemes, the Extended Speech Assessment Methods Phonetic Alphabet (X-SAMPA)symbols, and the corresponding visemes for the Korean voice supported by Amazon Polly.

IPA	X-SAMPA	Description	Example	Viseme
Consonants				
k	k	voiceless velar plosive	, [g]ang	k
k	k_t	strong voiceless velar plosive	, [kk]e	k
n	n	alveolar nasal	, [n]am	t
t	t	voiceless alveolar plosive	, [d]o	t
t	t_t	strong voiceless alveolar plosive	, [tt]e	t
	4	alveolar flap	, sa[r]ang	t
l	l	alveolar lateral approximant	, do[l]	t
m	m	bilabial nasal	, [m]u	p
p	p	voiceless bilabial plosive	, [b]om	p
p	p_t	strong voiceless bilabial plosive	, [pp]eol	p
s	s	voiceless alveolar fricative	, [s]e	s
s	s_t	strong voiceless alveolar fricative	, [ss]i	s
ŋ	N	velar nasal	, ba[ng]	k
t	ts\	voiceless alveolo-palatal affricate	, [j]o	J
t	ts_t	strong voiceless alveolo-palatal affricate	, [jj]i	J
t	ts_h	aspirated voiceless alveolo-palatal affricate	, [ch]a	J
k	k_h	aspirated voiceless velar plosive	, [k]o	k
t	t_h	aspirated voiceless alveolar plosive	, [t]ong	t
p	p_h	aspirated voiceless bilabial plosive	, [p]e	p
h	h	voiceless glottal fricative	, [h]im	k
j	j	palatal approximant	, [y]ang	i
w	w	labial-velar approximant	, [w]ang	u
	M\	velar approximant>	, [wj]i	i

IPA	X-SAMPA	Description	Example	Viseme
Vowels				
a	a	open front unrounded vowel	, b[a]b	a
	V	open-mid back unrounded vowel	, j[eo]ng	E
	E	open-mid front unrounded vowel	, b[e]	E
o	o	close-mid back rounded vowel	, n[o]	o
u	u	close back rounded vowel	, d[u]l	u
	M	close back unrounded vowel	, [eu]n	i
i	i	close front unrounded vowel	, k[i]m	i

Norwegian (nb-NO)

The following chart lists the full set of International Phonetic Alphabet (IPA) phonemes and the Extended Speech Assessment Methods Phonetic Alphabet (X-SAMPA) symbols as well as the corresponding visemes as supported by Amazon Polly for Norwegian language voices.

IPA	X-SAMPA	Description	Example	Viseme
Consonants				
	4	alveolar flap	pr**ø**v	t
b	b	voiced bilabial plosive	la**bb**	p
ç	C	voiceless palatal fricative	**k**ino	k
d	d	voiced alveolar plosive	la**dd**	t
	d'	voiced retroflex plosive	ver**d**i	t
f	f	voiceless labiodental fricative	**f**ot	f
		voiced velar plosive	ta**gg**	k
h	h	voiceless glottal fricative	**h**a	k
j	j	palatal approximant	**g**i	i
k	k	voiceless velar plosive	ta**kk**	k
l	l	alveolar lateral approximant	fa**ll**, ba**ll**	t
	l'	retroflex lateral approximant	æ**rl**ig	t
m	m	bilabial nasal	la**m**	p
n	n	alveolar nasal	va**nn**	t
	n'	retroflex nasal	ga**rn**	t
ŋ	N	velar nasal	sa**ng**	k
p	p	voiceless bilabial plosive	ho**pp**	p
s	s	voiceless alveolar fricative	la**ss**	s
	s'	voiceless retroflex fricative	å**rs**	S
	S	voiceless postalveolar fricative	**sk**yt	S
t	t	voiceless alveolar plosive	la**t**	t
	t'	voiceless retroflex plosive	har**dt**	t
	v\	labiodental approximant	**v**in	f
w	w	labial-velar approximant	**w**ill	x
Vowels				

IPA	X-SAMPA	Description	Example	Viseme
ø	2:	long close-mid front rounded vowel	søt	o
œ	9	open-mid front rounded vowel	søtt	O
ə	@	mid central vowel	ape	@
æ	{:	long near-open front unrounded vowel	vær	a
	}	close central rounded vowel	lund	u
	}:	long close central rounded vowel	lun	u
æ	{	near-open front unrounded vowel	vært	a
	A	open back unrounded vowel	hatt	a
	A:	long open back unrounded vowel	hat	a
e:	e:	long close-mid front unrounded vowel	sen	e
	E	open-mid front unrounded vowel	send	E
i:	i:	long close front unrounded vowel	vin	i
	I	near-close near-front unrounded vowel	vind	i
o	o	long close-mid back rounded vowel	våt	o
	O	open-mid back rounded vowel	vått	O
u:	u:	long close back rounded vowel	bok	u
	U	near-close near-back rounded vowel	bukk	u
y:	y:	long close front rounded vowel	lyn	u
	Y	near-close near-front rounded vowel	lynne	u

Polish (pl-PL)

The following table lists the International Phonetic Alphabet (IPA) phonemes, the Extended Speech Assessment Methods Phonetic Alphabet (X-SAMPA) symbols, and the corresponding visemes for the Polish voices that are supported by Amazon Polly.

Phoneme/Viseme Table

IPA	X-SAMPA	Description	Example	Viseme
Consonants				
b	b	voiced bilabial plosive	bobas, belka	p
d	d	voiced alveolar plosive	dar, do	t
dz	dz	voiced alveolar affricate	dzwon, widzowie	s
d	dz\	voiced alveolo-palatal affricate	dźwięk	J
d	dz'	voiced retroflex affricate	dżem, dżungla	S
f	f	voiceless labiodental fricative	furtka, film	f
g	g	voiced velar plosive	gazeta, waga	k
h	h	voiceless glottal fricative	chleb, handel	k
j	j	palatal approximant	jak, maja	i
k	k	voiceless velar plosive	kura, marek	k
l	l	alveolar lateral approximant	lipa, alicja	t
m	m	bilabial nasal	matka, molo	p
n	n	alveolar nasal	norka	t
	J	palatal nasal	koń, toruń	J
p	p	voiceless bilabial plosive	pora, stop	p
r	r	alveolar trill	rok, park	r
s	s	voiceless alveolar fricative	sum, pas	s
	s\	voiceless alveolo-palatal fricative	śruba, śnieg	J
	s'	voiceless retroflex fricative	szum, masz	S
t	t	voiceless alveolar plosive	tok, stół	t
ts	ts	voiceless alveolar affricate	car, co	s
t	ts\	voiceless alveolo-palatal affricate	ćma, mieć	J
t	ts'	voiceless retroflex affricate	czas, raczej	S
v	v	voiced labiodental fricative	worek, mewa	f

67

IPA	X-SAMPA	Description	Example	Viseme
w	w	labial-velar approximant	łaska, mało	u
z	z	voiced alveolar fricative	zero	s
	z\	voiced alveolo-palatal fricative	źrebię, bieliźnie	J
	zʻ	voiced retroflex fricative	żar, żona	S
Vowels				
a	a	open front unrounded vowel	ja	a
	E	open-mid front unrounded vowel	echo	E
~	E~	nasal open-mid front unrounded vowel	węże	E
i	i	close front unrounded vowel	ile	i
	O	open-mid back rounded vowel	oczy	O
~	O~	nasal open-mid back rounded vowel	wąż	O
u	u	close back rounded vowel	uczta	u
	1	close central unrounded vowel	byk	i

Portuguese (pt-PT)

The following table lists the International Phonetic Alphabet (IPA) phonemes, the Extended Speech Assessment Methods Phonetic Alphabet (X-SAMPA) symbols, and the corresponding visemes for the Portuguese voices that are supported by Amazon Polly.

Phoneme/Viseme Table

IPA	X-SAMPA	Description	Example	Viseme
Consonants				
	4	alveolar flap	pira	t
b	b	voiced bilabial plosive	dato	p
d	d	voiced alveolar plosive	dato	t
f	f	voiceless labiodental fricative	facto	f
g	g	voiced velar plosive	gato	k
j	j	palatal approximant	paraguay	i
k	k	voiceless velar plosive	cacto	k
l	l	alveolar lateral approximant	galo	t
	L	palatal lateral approximant	galho	J
m	m	bilabial nasal	mato	p
n	n	alveolar nasal	nato	t
	J	palatal nasal	pinha	J
p	p	voiceless bilabial plosive	pato	p
	R\	uvular trill	barroso	k
s	s	voiceless alveolar fricative	saca	s
	S	voiceless postalveolar fricative	chato	S
t	t	voiceless alveolar plosive	tacto	t
v	v	voiced labiodental fricative	vaca	f
w	w	labial-velar approximant	mau	u
z	z	voiced alveolar fricative	zaca	s
	Z	voiced postalveolar fricative	jacto	S
Vowels				
a	a	open front unrounded vowel	parto	a
ã	a~	nasal open front unrounded vowel	pega	a
e	e	close-mid front unrounded vowel	pega	e

69

IPA	X-SAMPA	Description	Example	Viseme
ẽ	e~	nasal close-mid front unrounded vowel	movem	e
	E	open-mid front unrounded vowel	café	E
i	i	close front unrounded vowel	lingueta	i
ĩ	i~	nasal close front unrounded vowel	cinto	i
o	o	close-mid back rounded vowel	poder	o
õ	o~	nasal close-mid back rounded vowel	compra	o
	O	open-mid back rounded vowel	cotó	O
u	u	close back rounded vowel	fui	u
ũ	u~	nasal close back rounded vowel	sunto	u

Portuguese, Brazilian (pt-BR)

The following table lists the International Phonetic Alphabet (IPA) phonemes, the Extended Speech Assessment Methods Phonetic Alphabet (X-SAMPA) symbols, and the corresponding visemes for the Brazilian Portuguese voices that are supported by Amazon Polly.

Phoneme/Viseme Table

IPA	X-SAMPA	Description	Example	Viseme
Consonants				
	4	alveolar flap	pi**r**a	t
b	b	voiced bilabial plosive	**b**ato	p
d	d	voiced alveolar plosive	**d**ato	t
d	dZ	voiced postalveolar affricate	ida**de**	S
f	f	voiceless labiodental fricative	**f**acto	f
g	g	voiced velar plosive	**g**ato	k
j	j	palatal approximant	parag**u**ay	i
k	k	voiceless velar plosive	**c**acto	k
l	l	alveolar lateral approximant	ga**l**o	t
	L	palatal lateral approximant	ga**lh**o	J
m	m	bilabial nasal	**m**ato	p
n	n	alveolar nasal	**n**ato	t
	J	palatal nasal	pi**nh**a	J
p	p	voiceless bilabial plosive	**p**ato	p
s	s	voiceless alveolar fricative	**s**aca	s
	S	voiceless postalveolar fricative	**ch**ato	S
t	t	voiceless alveolar plosive	**t**acto	t
t	tS	voiceless postalveolar affricate	no**it**e	S
v	v	voiced labiodental fricative	**v**aca	f
w	w	labial-velar approximant	ma**u**	u
	X	voiceless uvular fricative	ca**rr**o	k
z	z	voiced alveolar fricative	**z**aca	s
	Z	voiced postalveolar fricative	**j**acto	S
Vowels				

IPA	X-SAMPA	Description	Example	Viseme
a	a	open front unrounded vowel	p**a**rto	a
ã	a~	nasal open front unrounded vowel	pens**a**mos	a
e	e	close-mid front unrounded vowel	p**e**ga	e
ẽ	e~	nasal close-mid front unrounded vowel	mov**e**m	e
	E	open-mid front unrounded vowel	caf**é**	E
i	i	close front unrounded vowel	l**i**ngueta	i
ĩ	i~	nasal close front unrounded vowel	c**i**nto	i
o	o	close-mid back rounded vowel	p**o**der	o
õ	o~	nasal close-mid back rounded vowel	c**o**mpra	o
	O	open-mid back rounded vowel	cot**ó**	O
u	u	close back rounded vowel	f**u**i	u
ũ	u~	nasal close back rounded vowel	s**u**nto	u

Romanian (ro-RO)

The following table lists the International Phonetic Alphabet (IPA) phonemes, the Extended Speech Assessment Methods Phonetic Alphabet (X-SAMPA) symbols, and the corresponding visemes for the Romanian voice supported by Amazon Polly.

Phoneme/Viseme Table

IPA	X-SAMPA	Description	Example	Viseme
Consonants				
b	b	voiced bilabial plosive	bubă	p
d	d	voiced alveolar plosive	după	t
d	dZ	voiced postalveolar affricate	george	S
f	f	voiceless labiodental fricative	afacere	f
g	g	voiced velar plosive	agriș	k
h	h	voiceless glottal fricative	harpă	k
j	j	palatal approximant	baie	i
k	k	voiceless velar plosive	coș	k
l	l	alveolar lateral approximant	lampa	t
m	m	bilabial nasal	mama	p
n	n	alveolar nasal	nor	t
p	p	voiceless bilabial plosive	pilă	p
r	r	alveolar trill	rampă	r
s	s	voiceless alveolar fricative	soare	s
	S	voiceless postalveolar fricative	mașină	S
t	t	voiceless alveolar plosive	tata	t
ts	ts	voiceless alveolar affricate	țară	s
t	tS	voiceless postalveolar affricate	ceai	S
v	v	voiced labiodental fricative	viață	f
w	w	labial-velar approximant	beau	u
z	z	voiced alveolar fricative	mozol	s
	Z	voiced postalveolar fricative	joacă	S
Vowels				
ə	@	mid central vowel	babă	@

IPA	X-SAMPA	Description	Example	Viseme
a	a	open front un-rounded vowel	casa	a
e	e	close-mid front un-rounded vowel	elan	e
ę	e_^	non-syllabic close-mid front unrounded vowel	beau	e
i	i	close front un-rounded vowel	mie	i
o	o	close-mid back rounded vo	oră	o
oa	o_^a	diphthong	oare	o
u	u	close back rounded vowel	unde	u
	1	close central un-rounded vowel	România	i

Russian (ru-RU)

The following table lists the International Phonetic Alphabet (IPA) phonemes, the Extended Speech Assessment Methods Phonetic Alphabet (X-SAMPA) symbols, and the corresponding visemes for the Russian voices that are supported by Amazon Polly.

Phoneme/Viseme Table

IPA	X-SAMPA	Description	Example	Viseme
Consonants				
b	b	voiced bilabial plosive		p
b	b'	palatalized voiced bilabial plosive		p
d	d	voiced alveolar plosive		t
d	d'	palatalized voiced alveolar plosive		t
f	f	voiceless labiodental fricative		f
f	f'	palatalized voiceless labiodental fricative		f
g	g	voiced velar plosive		k
	g'	palatalized voiced velar plosive		k
j	j	palatal approximant	,	i
k	k	voiceless velar plosive		k
k	k'	palatalized voiceless velar plosive		k
l	l	alveolar lateral approximant		t
l	l'	palatalized alveolar lateral approximant		t
m	m	bilabial nasal		p
m	m'	palatalized bilabial nasal		p
n	n	alveolar nasal		t
n	n'	palatalized alveolar nasal		t
p	p	voiceless bilabial plosive		p
p	p'	palatalized voiceless bilabial plosive		p
r	r	alveolar trill		r
r	r'	palatalized alveolar trill		r
s	s	voiceless alveolar fricative		s

IPA	X-SAMPA	Description	Example	Viseme
s	s'	palatalized voiceless alveolar fricative	,	s
ː	s\:	long voiceless alveolo-palatal fricative		J
	s'	voiceless retroflex fricative		S
t	t	voiceless alveolar plosive		t
t	t'	palatalized voiceless alveolar plosive		t
ts	ts	voiceless alveolar affricate		s
t	ts\	voiceless alveolo-palatal affricate		J
v	v	voiced labiodental fricative		f
v	v'	palatalized voiced labiodental fricative		f
x	x	voiceless velar fricative		k
x	x'	palatalized voiceless velar fricative		k
z	z	voiced alveolar fricative		s
z	z'	palatalized voiced alveolar fricative		s
ː	z\:	long voiced alveolo-palatal fricative		J
	z'	voiced retroflex fricative		S
Vowels				
ə	@	mid central vowel		@
a	a	open front unrounded vowel	,	a
e	e	close-mid front unrounded vowel		e
	E	open-mid front unrounded vowel		E
i	i	close front unrounded vowel	,	i
o	o	close-mid back rounded vowel		o
u	u	close back rounded vowel	,	u
	1	close central unrounded vowel		i

Spanish (es-ES)

The following table lists the International Phonetic Alphabet (IPA) phonemes, the Extended Speech Assessment Methods Phonetic Alphabet (X-SAMPA) symbols, and the corresponding visemes for the Spanish voices that are supported by Amazon Polly.

Phoneme/Viseme Table

IPA	X-SAMPA	Description	Example	Viseme
Consonants				
	4	alveolar flap	pero, bravo, amor, eterno	t
b	b	voiced bilabial plosive	bestia	p
	B	voiced bilabial fricative	bebé	B
d	d	voiced alveolar plosive	cuando	t
ð	D	voiced dental fricative	arder	T
f	f	voiceless labiodental fricative	fase, café	f
g	g	voiced velar plosive	gato, lengua, guerra	k
	G	voiced velar fricative	trigo, Argos	k
j	j	palatal approximant	hacia, tierra, radio, viuda	i
	j\	voiced palatal fricative	enhielar, sayo, inyectado, desyerba	J
k	k	voiceless velar plosive	caña, laca, quisimos	k
l	l	alveolar lateral approximant	lino, calor, principal	t
	L	palatal lateral approximant	llave, pollo	J
m	m	bilabial nasal	madre, comer, anfibio	p
n	n	alveolar nasal	nido, anillo, sin	t
	J	palatal nasal	cabaña, ñoquis	J
ŋ	N	velar nasal	cinco, venga	k
p	p	voiceless bilabial plosive	pozo, topo	p
r	r	alveolar trill	perro, enrachado	r
s	s	voiceless alveolar fricative	saco, casa, puertas	s
t	t	voiceless alveolar plosive	tamiz, átomo	t
t	tS	voiceless postalveolar affricate	chubasco	S
	T	voiceless dental fricative	cereza, zorro, lacero, paz	T

IPA	X-SAMPA	Description	Example	Viseme
w	w	labial-velar approximant	fuego, fuimos, cuota, cuadro	u
x	x	voiceless velar fricative	jamón, general, suje, reloj	k
z	z	voiced alveolar fricative	rasgo, mismo	s
Vowels				
a	a	open front unrounded vowel	tanque	a
e	e	close-mid front unrounded vowel	peso	e
i	i	close front unrounded vowel	cinco	i
o	o	close-mid back rounded vowel	bosque	o
u	u	close-mid front unrounded vowel	publicar	u
e	e	close-mid front unrounded vowel	keçi	e
	E	open-mid front unrounded vowel	dede	e
i	i	close front unrounded vowel	bir	i
i:	i:	long close front unrounded vowel	izah	i
	I	near-close near-front unrounded vowel	keçi	i
	M	close back unrounded vowel	kıl	i
o	o	long close-mid back rounded vowel	kol	o
o:	o:	long close-mid back rounded vowel	dolar	o
u	u	close back rounded vowel	durum	u
u:	u:	long close back rounded vowel	ruhum	u
	U	near-close near-back rounded vowel	dolu	u
Y	y	close front rounded vowel	güvenlik	u
	Y	near-close near-front rounded vowel	aşı	u

Spanish, US (es-US)

The following table lists the International Phonetic Alphabet (IPA) phonemes, the Extended Speech Assessment Methods Phonetic Alphabet (X-SAMPA) symbols, and the corresponding visemes for the US Spanish voices that are supported by Amazon Polly.

IPA	X-SAMPA	Description	Example	Viseme
Consonants				
b	b	Voiced bilabial plosive	bed	p
d	d	Voiced alveolar plosive	dig	t
d	dZ	Voiced postalveolar affricate	jump	S
ð	D	Voiced dental fricative	then	T
f	f	Voiceless labiodental fricative	five	f
g	g	Voiced velar plosive	game	k
h	h	Voiceless glottal fricative	house	k
j	j	Palatal approximant	yes	i
k	k	Voiceless velar plosive	cat	k
l	l	Alveolar lateral approximant	lay	t
m	m	Bilabial nasal	mouse	p
n	n	Alveolar nasal	nap	t
ŋ	N	Velar nasal	thing	k
p	p	Voiceless bilabial plosive	speak	p
	r\	Alveolar approximant	red	r
s	s	Voiceless alveolar fricative	seem	s
	S	Voiceless postalveolar fricative	ship	S
t	t	Voiceless alveolar plosive	trap	t
t	tS	Voiceless postalveolar affricate	chart	S
Θ	T	Voiceless dental fricative	thin	T
v	v	Voiced labiodental fricative	vest	f
w	w	Labial-velar approximant	west	u
z	z	Voiced alveolar fricative	zero	s
	Z	Voiced postalveolar fricative	vision	S
Vowels				

IPA	X-SAMPA	Description	Example	Viseme
ə	@	Mid central vowel	arena	@
	@'	Mid central r-colored vowel	reader	@
æ	{	Near open-front unrounded vowel	trap	a
a	aI	Diphthong	price	a
a	aU	Diphthong	mouth	a
	A	Long open-back unrounded vowel	father	a
e	eI	Diphthong	face	e
	3'	Open mid-central unrounded r-colored vowel	nurse	E
	E	Open mid-front unrounded vowel	dress	E
i:	i	Long close front unrounded vowel	fleece	i
	I	Near-close near-front unrounded vowel	kit	i
o	oU	Diphthong	goat	o
	O	Long open mid-back rounded vowel	thought	O
	OI	Diphthong	choice	O
u	u	Long close-back rounded vowel	goose	u
	U	Near-close near-back rounded vowel	foot	u
	V	Open-mid-back unrounded vowel	strut	E

Swedish (sv-SE)

The following table lists the International Phonetic Alphabet (IPA) phonemes, the Extended Speech Assessment Methods Phonetic Alphabet (X-SAMPA) symbols, and the corresponding visemes for the Swedish voice supported by Amazon Polly.

Phoneme/Viseme Table

IPA	X-SAMPA	Description	Example	Viseme
Consonants				
b	b	voiced bilabial plosive	**b**il	p
d	d	voiced alveolar plosive	**d**al	t
	dʻ	voiced retroflex plosive	bo**rd**	t
f	f	voiceless labiodental fricative	**f**il	f
g	g	voiced velar plosive	**g**ås	k
h	h	voiceless glottal fricative	**h**al	k
j	j	palatal approximant	**j**ag	i
k	k	voiceless velar plosive	**k**al	k
l	l	alveolar lateral approximant	**l**ös	t
	lʻ	retroflex lateral approximant	hä**rl**ig	t
m	m	bilabial nasal	**m**il	p
n	n	alveolar nasal	**n**ålar	t
	nʻ	retroflex nasal	ba**rn**	t
ŋ	N	velar nasal	ri**ng**	k
p	p	voiceless bilabial plosive	**p**il	p
r	r	alveolar trill	**r**is	r
s	s	voiceless alveolar fricative	**s**il	s
	s\	voiceless alveolo-palatal fricative	**tj**ock	J
	sʻ	voiceless retroflex fricative	fo**rs**, **sch**lager	S
t	t	voiceless alveolar plosive	**t**al	t
	tʻ	voiceless retroflex plosive	**hj**ort	t
v	v	voiced labiodental fricative	**v**år	f
w	w	labial-velar approximant	a**u**la, a**i**rways	u
	x\	voiceless palatal-velar fricative	**sj**uk	k
Vowels				

IPA	X-SAMPA	Description	Example	Viseme
ø	2	close-mid front rounded vowel	föll, förr	o
ø	2:	long close-mid front rounded vowel	föl, nöt, för	o
	8	close-mid central rounded vowel	buss, full	o
ə	@	mid central vowel	pojken	@
	}:	long close central rounded vowel	hus, ful	u
a	a	open front un-rounded vowel	hall, matt	a
æ	{	near-open front unrounded vowel	herr	a
	A:	long open back un-rounded vowel	hal, mat	a
e:	e:	long close-mid front unrounded vowel	vet, hel	e
	E	open-mid front unrounded vowel	vett, rätt, hetta, häll	E
	E:	long open-mid front unrounded vowel	säl, häl, här	E:
i:	i:	long close front unrounded vowel	vit, sil	i:
	I	near-close near-front unrounded vowel	vitt, sill	i
o:	o:	long close-mid back rounded vowel	hål, mål	o
	O	open-mid back rounded vowel	håll, moll	O
u:	u:	long close back rounded vowel	sol, bot	u
	U	near-close near-back rounded vowel	bott	u
y	y	close front rounded vowel	bytt	u
y:	y:	long close front rounded vowel	syl, syl	u

82

Turkish (tr-TR)

The following table lists the International Phonetic Alphabet (IPA) phonemes, the Extended Speech Assessment Methods Phonetic Alphabet (X-SAMPA) symbols, and the corresponding visemes for the Turkish voice supported by Amazon Polly.

Phoneme/Viseme Table

IPA	X-SAMPA	Description	Example	Viseme
Consonants				
	4	alveolar flap	durum	t
°	4_0_r	voiceless fricated alveolar flap	bir	t
	4_r	fricated alveolar flap	raf	t
b	b	voiced bilabial plosive	raf	p
c	c	voiceless palatal plosive	kedi	k
d	d	voiced alveolar plosive	dede	t
d	dZ	voiced postalveolar affricate	cam	S
f	f	voiceless labiodental fricative	fare	f
g	g	voiced velar plosiv	galibi	k
h	h	voiceless glottal fricative	hasta	k
j	j	palatal approximant	yat	i
	J\	voiced palatal plosive	genç	J
k	k	voiceless velar plosive	akıl	k
l	l	alveolar lateral approximant	lale	t
	5	velarized alveolar lateral approximant	labirent	t
m	m	bilabial nasal	maaş	p
n	n	alveolar nasal	anı	t
p	p	voiceless bilabial plosive	ip	p
s	s	voiceless alveolar fricative	ses	s
	S	voiceless postalveolar fricative	aşı	S
t	t	voiceless alveolar plosive	ütü	t
t	tS	voiceless postalveolar affricate	çaba	S
v	v	voiced labiodental fricative	ekvator, kahveci, akvaryum, isveçli, teşviki, cetvel	f

IPA	X-SAMPA	Description	Example	Viseme
z	z	voiced alveolar fricative	ver	s
	Z	voiced postalveolar fricative	azık	S
Vowels				
ø	2	close-mid front rounded vowel	göl	0
œ	9	open-mid front rounded vowel	banliyö	O
a	a	open front unrounded vowel	kal	a
a:	a:	long open front unrounded vowel	davacı	a
æ	{	near-open front unrounded vowel	özlem, güvenlik, gürel, somersault	a
e	e	close-mid front unrounded vowel	keçi	e
	E	open-mid front unrounded vowel	dede	E
i	i	close front unrounded vowel	bir	i
i:	i:	long close front unrounded vowel	izah	i
	I	near-close near-front unrounded vowel	keçi	i
	M	close back unrounded vowel	kıl	i
o	o	close-mid back rounded vowel	kol	o
o:	o:	long close-mid back rounded vowel	dolar	o
u	u	close back rounded vowel	durum	u
u:	u:	long close back rounded vowel	ruhum	u
	U	near-close near-back rounded vowel	dolu	u
y	y	close front rounded vowel	güvenlik	u
	Y	near-close near-front rounded vowel	aşı	u

Welsh (cy-GB)

The following table lists the International Phonetic Alphabet (IPA) phonemes, the Extended Speech Assessment Methods Phonetic Alphabet (X-SAMPA) symbols, and the corresponding visemes for the Welsh voice supported by Amazon Polly.

Phoneme/Viseme Table

IPA	X-SAMPA	Description	Example	Viseme
Consonants				
b	b	voiced bilabial plosive	baban	p
d	d	voiced alveolar plosive	deg	t
d	dZ	voiced postalveolar affricate	garej	S
ð	D	voiced dental fricative	deuddeg	T
f	f	voiceless labiodental fricative	ffacs	f
g	g	voiced velar plosive	gadael	k
h	h	voiceless glottal fricative	haearn	k
j	j	palatal approximant	astudio	i
k	k	voiceless velar plosive	cant	k
l	l	alveolar lateral approximant	lan	t
	K	voiceless alveolar lateral fricative	llan	t
m	m	bilabial nasal	mae	p
m	m_0	voiceless bilabial nasal	ymhen	p
n	n	alveolar nasal	naw	t
n	n_0	voiceless alveolar nasal	anhawster	t
ŋ	N	velar nasal	argyfwng	k
ŋ̊	N_0	voiceless velar nasal	anghenion	k
p	p	voiceless bilabial plosive	pump	p
r	r	alveolar trill	rhoi	r
r	r_0	voiceless alveolar trill	garw	r
s	s	voiceless alveolar fricative	saith	s
	S	voiceless postalveolar fricative	siawns	S
t	t	voiceless alveolar plosive	tegan	t
t	tS	voiceless postalveolar affricate	cytsain	S

IPA	X-SAMPA	Description	Example	Viseme
	T	voiceless dental fricative	aber**th**	T
v	v	voiced labiodental fricative	praw**f**	f
w	w	labial-velar ap-proximant	rhag**w**eld	u
	X	voiceless uvular fricative	**ch**we**ch**	k
z	z	voiced alveolar fricative	aid**s**	s
	Z	voiced postalveo-lar fricative	rou**ge**	S
Vowels				
ə	@	mid central vowel	**y**chwaneg**a**	@
a	a	open front un-rounded vowel	**a**cen	a
ai	ai	diphthong	d**au**	a
au	au	diphthong	**aw**dur	a
	A:	long open back un-rounded vowel	m**a**b	a
	A:1	diphthong	**ae**lod	a
e:	e:	long close-mid front unrounded vowel	p**e**th	e
	E	open-mid front unrounded vowel	p**e**dwar	E
i	Ei	diphthong	b**ei**c	E
i:	i:	long close front unrounded vowel	tr**i**	i
	I	near-close near-front unrounded vowel	m**i**liwn	i
u	1u	diphthong	unigr**yw**	i
o:	o:	long close-mid back rounded vowel	**o**ddi	o
	O	open-mid back rounded vowel	**o**ddieithr	O
i	Oi	diphthong	tr**oi**	O
u	Ou	diphthong	r**ow**nd	O
u:	u:	long close back rounded vowel	c**w**ch	u
	U	near-close near-back rounded vowel	a**cw**stig	u
i	Ui	diphthong	**wy**th	u

Using SSML

Amazon Polly generates speech from both plain text input and Speech Synthesis Markup Language (SSML) documents that conform to SSML version 1.1. Using SSML tags, you can customize and control aspects of speech such as pronunciation, volume, and speech rate.

Amazon Polly supports SSML 1.1 as defined in the following W3C recommendation:

- Speech Synthesis Markup Language (SSML) Version 1.1, W3C Recommendation 7 September 2010

Some of the elements in the SSML W3C recommendation are not supported. For more information, see Limits in Amazon Polly.

This section provides simple examples of SSML that can be used to generate and control speech output. The examples also provide the `synthesize-speech` AWS CLI command to test these examples.

- Using SSML with the Amazon Polly Console
- Using SSML with the AWS CLI
- SSML Tags in Amazon Polly

Using SSML with the Amazon Polly Console

Amazon Polly supports version 1.1 SSML as defined by the W3C. This section covers how to use SSML input for speech synthesis in the Amazon Polly console.

Using SSML with the Amazon Polly Console

The following procedure synthesizes speech using SSML input. Except for steps 3 and 4 below, the steps in this example are identical to those in Exercise 2: Synthesizing Speech (Plain Text Input).

To synthesize speech using the Amazon Polly console (SSML input)

In this example we introduce SSML tagging to substitute "World Wide Web Consortium" for "W3C". Compare the results of this exercise with that of Applying Lexicons Using the Console (Synthesize Speech) for both US English and another language.

1. Sign in to the AWS Management Console and open the Amazon Polly console at https://console.aws. amazon.com/polly/.

2. If needed, choose the **Text-to-Speech** tab.

3. Choose the **SSML** tab.

4. Type or paste the following text in the text box:

```
1  <speak>
2      He was caught up in the game.<break time="1s"/>
3      In the middle of the 10/3/2014 <sub alias="World Wide Web Consortium">W3C</sub>
           meeting
4      he shouted, "Score!" quite loudly. When his boss stared at him, he repeated
5      <amazon:effect name="whispered">"Score"</amazon:effect> in a whisper.
6  </speak>
```

The SSML tags inform Amazon Polly that the text should be rendered in a specified way.

- `<break time="1s"/>` instructs Amazon Polly to pause 1 second between the initial two sentences.

- `<sub alias="World Wide Web Consortium">W3C</sub>` instructs Amazon Polly to substitute "World Wide Web Consortium" for the acronym "W3C".

- `<amazon:effect name="whispered">Score</amazon:effect>` instructs Amazon Polly to say the second "Score" in a whispered voice.

For more information on SSML with examples, see Supported SSML Tags

5. For **Choose a language and region**, choose **English US**, then choose the voice you want.

6. To listen to the speech immediately, choose **Listen to speech**.

7. To save the speech file, choose **Download [format]** if the format is the one you want. Otherwise choose **Change file format**, choose the format you want, and then choose **Change**. Choose **Download [format]**.

Related Console Examples

- Exercise 2: Synthesizing Speech (Plain Text Input)

- Applying Lexicons Using the Console (Synthesize Speech)

Note
When entering the input text in the AWS CLI, quotation marks are used around the input text to differentiate

it from the surrounding code. Because the Amazon Polly console does not show you the code, quotation marks are not used around the input text in the console.

Next Step

Applying Lexicons Using the Console (Synthesize Speech)

Using SSML with the AWS CLI

The following topics demonstrate how to use SSML input with the AWS CLI for Amazon Polly.

Example 1: Passing SSML Through the Synthesize-Speech Command

In the following `synthesize-speech` command, you specify a simple SSML string with only the required opening and closing `<speak></speak>` tags and the quotation marks that surround them. (Optionally, you can specify the full document header too). Because plain text is the default, the command also specifies the `--text-type` parameter to indicate that the input text is SSML. The only required elements for an SSML string are the input text (targeted by the generated speech), `output-format`, and `voice-id`.

Important

Although you do not use quotation marks around the input text in the Amazon Polly Console, they are required when using the AWS CLI or other code, both for plain text and SSML. It is also important that the quotation marks around the entire input text and the quotation marks within the text are differentiated.

For example, you can use single quote marks (') surrounding the entire input text, and standard quotation marks (") in any interior tags or use the reverse. (When using the AWS CLI, both options will work for Unix, Linux, and macOS. Standard quotations marks for the input text and single quote marks for interior tags are required when using a Windows command prompt.)

Thus you can use either

```
1 --text '<speak>Hello <break time="300ms"/> World</speak>'
```

or

```
1 --text "<speak>Hello <break time='300ms'/> World</speak>"
```

The following AWS CLI example is formatted for Unix, Linux, and macOS. For Windows, replace the backslash (\) Unix continuation character at the end of each line with a caret (^) and use full quotation marks (") around the input text with single quotes (') for interior tags.

```
1 aws polly synthesize-speech \
2 --text-type ssml \
3 --text '<speak>Hello world</speak>' \
4 --output-format mp3 \
5 --voice-id Joanna \
6 speech.mp3
```

Play the resulting `speech.mp3` file to verify the synthesized speech.

Example 2: Synthesizing a Full SSML Document

In this example you save SSML content to a file and specify the file name in the `synthesize-speech` command. This example uses the following SSML.

```
1 <?xml version="1.0"?>
2 <speak version="1.1"
3     xmlns="http://www.w3.org/2001/10/synthesis"
4     xmlns:xsi="http://www.w3.org/2001/XMLSchema-instance"
5     xsi:schemaLocation="http://www.w3.org/2001/10/synthesis http://www.w3.org/TR/speech-
            synthesis11/synthesis.xsd"
6     xml:lang="en-US">Hello World</speak>
```

Note that the `xml:lang` attribute specifies `en-US` (US English) as the language of the input text. For information about how the language of the input text and the language of the voice selected affect the `SynthesizeSpeech` operation, see Using the xml:lang Attribute.

To test the SSML

1. Save the SSML to a file (`example.xml`).

2. Run the following `synthesize-speech` command from the path where the XML file is stored and specify the SSML as input. Note that because this points to a file rather than containing the actual input text, no quotation marks are needed.

   The following AWS CLI example is formatted for Unix, Linux, and macOS. For Windows, replace the backslash (\) Unix continuation character at the end of each line with a caret (^) and use full quotation marks (") around the input text with single quotes (') for interior tags.

```
1 aws polly synthesize-speech \
2 --text-type ssml \
3 --text file://example.xml \
4 --output-format mp3 \
5 --voice-id Joanna \
6 speech.mp3
```

3. Play the `speech.mp3` file to verify the synthesized speech.

Example 3: Using Common SSML Tags

This section explains how to use some common SSML tags to achieve specific results. For more examples, see Speech Synthesis Markup Language (SSML) Version 1.1.

You can use the `synthesize-speech` command to test the examples in this section.

Using the Element

The following SSML `synthesize-speech` command uses the `<break>` element to add a 300 millisecond delay between the words "Hello" and "World" in the resulting speech.

```
1 <speak>
2     Hello <break time="300ms"/> World.
3 </speak>
```

The following AWS CLI example is formatted for Unix, Linux, and macOS. For Windows, replace the backslash (\) Unix continuation character at the end of each line with a caret (^) and use full quotation marks (") around the input text with single quotes (') for interior tags.

```
1 aws polly synthesize-speech \
2 --text-type ssml \
3 --text '<speak>Hello <break time="300ms"/> World</speak>' \
4 --output-format mp3 \
5 --voice-id Joanna \
6 speech.mp3
```

Play the resulting `speech.mp3` file to verify the synthesized speech.

Using the Element

This element enables you to control pitch, speaking rate, and volume of speech.

- The following SSML uses the `<prosody>` element to control volume:

```
1 <speak>
2     <prosody volume="+20dB">Hello world</prosody>
3 </speak>
```

The following AWS CLI example is formatted for Unix, Linux, and macOS. For Windows, replace the backslash (\) Unix continuation character at the end of each line with a caret (^) and use full quotation marks (") around the input text with single quotes (') for interior tags.

```
1 aws polly synthesize-speech \
2 --text-type ssml \
3 --text '<speak><prosody volume="+20dB">Hello world</prosody></speak>' \
4 --output-format mp3 \
5 --voice-id Joanna \
6 speech.mp3
```

- The following SSML uses the `<prosody>` element to control pitch:

```
1 <speak>
2     <prosody pitch="x-high">Hello world.</prosody>
3 </speak>
```

The following AWS CLI example is formatted for Unix, Linux, and macOS. For Windows, replace the backslash (\) Unix continuation character at the end of each line with a caret (^) and use full quotation marks (") around the input text with single quotes (') for interior tags.

```
1 aws polly synthesize-speech \
2 --text-type ssml \
3 --text '<speak><prosody pitch="x-high">Hello world</prosody></speak>' \
4 --output-format mp3 \
5 --voice-id Joanna \
6 speech.mp3
```

- The following SSML uses the `<prosody>` element to specify the speech rate:

```
1 <speak>
2     <prosody rate="x-fast">Hello world.</prosody>
3 </speak>
```

The following AWS CLI example is formatted for Unix, Linux, and macOS. For Windows, replace the backslash (\) Unix continuation character at the end of each line with a caret (^) and use full quotation marks (") around the input text with single quotes (') for interior tags.

```
1 aws polly synthesize-speech \
2 --text-type ssml \
3 --text '<speak><prosody rate="x-fast">Hello world</prosody></speak>' \
4 --output-format mp3 \
5 --voice-id Joanna \
6 speech.mp3
```

- You can specify multiple attributes in a `<prosody>` element, as shown in the following example:

```
1 <speak>
2     <prosody volume="x-loud" pitch="x-high" rate="x-fast">Hello world.</prosody>
3 </speak>
```

The following AWS CLI example is formatted for Unix, Linux, and macOS. For Windows, replace the backslash (\) Unix continuation character at the end of each line with a caret (^) and use full quotation marks (") around the input text with single quotes (') for interior tags.

```
1 aws polly synthesize-speech \
2 --text-type ssml \
3 --text '<speak><prosody volume="x-loud" pitch="x-high" rate="x-fast">Hello world</prosody
    ></speak>' \
4 --output-format mp3 \
5 --voice-id Joanna \
6 speech.mp3
```

Play the resulting `speech.mp3` file to verify the synthesized speech.

Using a whispered voice

The following synthesize-speech command uses the `<amazon:effect name="whispered">` element to say the words "little lamb" in a whispered voice in the resulting speech:

```
1 <speak>
2     Mary has a <amazon:effect name="whispered">little lamb.</amazon:effect>
3 </speak>
```

This effect can be enhanced by slowing the whispered speech slightly using the element.

The following AWS CLI example is formatted for Unix, Linux, and macOS. For Windows, replace the backslash (\) Unix continuation character at the end of each line with a caret (^) and use full quotation marks (") around the input text with single quotes (') for interior tags.

```
1 aws polly synthesize-speech \
2 --text-type ssml \
3 --text '<speak> Mary has a <prosody rate="-10%"><amazon:effect name="whispered"> \
4 little lamb.</amazon:effect></prosody></speak>' \
5 --output-format mp3 \
6 --voice-id Joanna \
7 speech.mp3
```

Play the resulting `speech.mp3` file to verify the synthesized speech.

Using the Element

This element enables you to specify the stress or prominence to apply when speaking a specified word or phrase.

```
1 <speak>
2     <emphasis level="strong">Hello</emphasis> world how are you?
3 </speak>
```

The following AWS CLI example is formatted for Unix, Linux, and macOS. For Windows, replace the backslash (\) Unix continuation character at the end of each line with a caret (^) and use full quotation marks (") around the input text with single quotes (') for interior tags.

```
1 aws polly synthesize-speech \
2 --text-type ssml \
3 --text '<speak><emphasis level="strong">Hello</emphasis> world how are you?</speak>' \
4 --output-format mp3 \
5 --voice-id Joanna \
6 speech.mp3
```

Play the resulting `speech.mp3` file to verify the synthesized speech.

Example 4: Controlling the Way Words are Said

This example explains some of the common SSML tags you can use to control the way Amazon Polly says certain words, either by interpreting the words in a particular way or by how they're pronounced.

Using the <say-as> Element

The <say-as> element enables you to provide information about the type of text contained within the element.

For instance, in the following SSML, `<say-as>` indicates that the text 4/6 should be interpreted in a specific way, the attribute `interpret-as="date" format="dm"` indicates it should be said as a date value with the format month/day.

```
1 <speak>
2     Today is <say-as interpret-as="date" format="md" >4/6</say-as>
3 </speak>
```

This element can also be used to say fractions, telephone numbers, measurement units, and more.

The following AWS CLI example is formatted for Unix, Linux, and macOS. For Windows, replace the backslash (\) Unix continuation character at the end of each line with a caret (^) and use full quotation marks (") around the input text with single quotes (') for interior tags.

```
1 aws polly synthesize-speech \
2 --text-type ssml \
3 --text '<speak>Today is <say-as interpret-as="date" format="md" >4/6</say-as></speak>' \
4 --output-format mp3 \
5 --voice-id Joanna \
6 speech.mp3
```

The resulting speech says "Today is June 4th". The `<say-as>` tag describes how the text should be interpreted by providing additional context via the `interpret-as` attribute.

Play the resulting `speech.mp3` file to verify the synthesized speech.

For more information on this element, see <say-as>.

Using the xml:lang Attribute

You can improve pronunciation of words that are foreign to the input text language by specifying the target language using the `xml:lang` attribute. This forces the TTS engine to apply different pronunciation rules for the words that are specific to the target language. The examples below show different combinations of languages for the input text and the voices you can specify in the `synthesize-speech` call. You can test these examples using the `synthesize-speech` command to verify the results.

For a complete list of which languages are available, see Languages Supported by Amazon Polly.

In this example, the chosen voice is a US English voice. Amazon Polly assumes the input text is in the same language as the selected voice. To achieve a Spanish pronunciation of specific words, you need to mark the targeted words as Spanish.

```
1 aws polly synthesize-speech \
2 --text-type ssml \
3 --text '<speak>That restaurant is terrific. <lang xml:lang="es-ES">Mucho gusto.</lang></speak>'
      \
```

```
4 --output-format mp3 \
5 --voice-id Joanna \
6 speech.mp3
```

Because the language of the input text is specified, Amazon Polly maps the resulting Spanish phonemes to English phonemes of the smallest acoustic distance. As a result, Salli reads the text as a US native speaker who knows the correct Spanish pronunciation, but in a US English accent.

Note

This practice is limited to pairs of languages available in the Amazon Polly language portfolio. Some language pairs work better than others because of the phonological structure of the languages.

Play the resulting `speech.mp3` file to listen to the synthesized speech.

SSML Tags in Amazon Polly

Using SSML-enhanced input text enables you to exert additional control over how Amazon Polly generates speech from the text you provide.

For example, you can include a long pause within your text, or alter it in another way such as changing the speech rate or pitch. Amazon Polly provides this type of control and more using a subset of the SSML markup tags as defined by Speech Synthesis Markup Language (SSML) Version 1.1, W3C Recommendation

Supported SSML Tags

Amazon Polly supports the following SSML:

root

-

standard tags

-
-
-
-
-
-
-
- <say-as>
-
-

Amazon Polly-specific tags

- <amazon:effect name="drc">
- <amazon:effect phonation="soft">
- <amazon:effect vocal-tract-length>
- <amazon:effect name="whispered">

Note that any SSML tags in your input text that are unsupported are automatically ignored when Amazon Polly processes it.

The `<speak>` tag is the root element of all Amazon Polly SSML text. All SSML-enhanced text to be spoken must be included within this tag.

```
1 <speak>Mary had a little lamb.</speak>
```

This tag indicates a pause in the speech. The length of the pause can be set with either a `strength` or `time` attribute. If no attribute is used with a `break` tag, the default `<break strength="medium">` is used.

The following values can be used with the `strength` attribute:

- `none`: No pause occurs. This can be used to remove a pause that would normally occur (such as after a period).
- `x-weak`: Same as `none`.
- `weak`: Treats adjacent words as if they are separated by a single comma.
- `medium`: Same as `weak`.
- `strong`: Treats adjacent words as if they are separated by a sentence break (equivalent to the `<s>` tag).
- `x-strong`: Treats adjacent words as if they are separated by a paragraphy break (equivalent to the `<p>` tag).

The following values can be used with the `time` attribute:

- `s`: Duration of the pause in seconds. A pause may be up to `10s` in duration.
- `ms`: Duration of the pause in milliseconds. A pause may be up to `10000ms`.

For example:

```
1  <speak>
2      Mary had a little lamb <break time="3s"/>Whose fleece was white as snow.
3  </speak>
```

This tag emphasizes the tagged words or phrases. Emphasizing text changes the rate and volume of the speech. More emphasis means the text is spoken louder and slower. Less emphasis is quieter and faster. The `level` attribute indicates the degree of emphasis that you want to place on the text.

Three `level` options are available:

- `Strong`: Increases the volume and slows down speaking rate so the speech is louder and slower.
- `Moderate`: Increases the volume and slows down the speaking rate, but less so than when set to `strong`. This is the default and is used if no level is provided.
- `Reduced`: Decrease the volume and speed up the speaking rate. The speech is softer and faster.

Note
The normal speaking rate and volume for a given voice will fall between the `moderate` and `reduced` levels.

For example:

```
1  <speak>
2      I already told you I <emphasis level="strong">really like</emphasis> that person.
3  </speak>
```

This tag indicates the language of a specific word or phrase. Foreign language words and phrases are generally rendered better audibly when they are enclosed in inside a `<lang>` tag. The language in which you want to render the pronunciation must be specified using the `xml:lang` attribute.

For a complete list of which languages are available, see Languages Supported by Amazon Polly.

The actual language in which the word or phrase is rendered is the language of the `voice-id` used, and not the language of the `<lang>` tag. The tag serves only to set the pronunciation of the text, when it is different from the language of the `voice-id`.

For example:

When the `voice-id` is Joanna (American English), run the following:

```
1 <speak>
2     Je ne parle pas français.
3 </speak>
```

Amazon Polly will say this in the Joanna voice without attempting to use a French accent.

When the same voice is used with the following `<lang>` tab:

```
1 <speak>
2     <lang xml:lang="fr-FR">Je ne parle pas français.</lang>.
3 </speak>
```

Amazon Polly will pronounce this in the Joanna voice using American-accented French.

However, because Joanna is not a native French voice, pronunciation is based on the language the voice speaks natively. For example, while a perfect French pronunciation would feature an uvual trill /R/ in the word adore, Joanna's American English voice will pronounce it as this phoneme as the corresponding sound /r/.

In another, when the `voice-id` of Giorgio (Italian) is used with the following text:

```
1 <speak>
2     Mi piace Bruce Springsteen.
3 </speak>
```

Amazon Polly will say this in the Giorgio voice with no attempt to use a non-Italian pronunciation.

When the same voice is used with the following `<lang>` tab:

```
1 <speak>
2     Mi piace <lang xml:lang="en-US">Bruce Springsteen.</lang>
3 </speak>
```

Amazon Polly will pronounce this in the Giorgio voice using Italian-accented English.

This tag provides the user with the ability to place a custom tag within the text. No action is taken on the tag by Amazon Polly, but when SSML metadata is returned, the position of this tag will also be returned.

This tag may be anything designated by the user with the following format:

```
1 <mark name="tag_name"/>
```

For example, if the tag name is "animal" and the input text is:

```
1 <speak>
2     Mary had a little <mark name="animal"/>lamb.
3 </speak>
```

the following SSML metadata might be returned by Amazon Polly

```
1 {"time":767,"type":"ssml","start":25,"end":46,"value":"animal"}
```

This tag indicates a paragraph in the text. This is equivalent to specifying a pause with `<break strength="x-strong"/>`. As with the `<s>` tag, this tag needs to enclose the sentence in question.

```
1 <speak>
2     <p>This is the first paragraph. There should be a pause after this text is spoken.</p>
3     <p>This is the second paragraph.</p>
4 </speak>
```

This tag provides a phonetic pronunciation (the phonemes) for the indicated text.

Two attributes are required with the `phoneme` tag:

- `alphabet`
  - `ipa` —Indicates the phoneme uses The International Phonetic Alphabet (IPA) system.
  - `x-sampa` —Indicates the phoneme uses The Extended Speech Assessment Methods Phonetic Alphabet (X-SAMPA) system.
- `ph`
  - Indicates the phonetic symbols to be used for pronunciation. Amazon Polly supports standard IPA and X-SAMPA phonetic symbols. For more information see Phonetic Tables Used by Amazon Polly

When using the `phoneme` tag, Amazon Polly uses the pronunciation provided in the `ph` attribute rather than the one associated by default with the text contained within the tags. However, you should still provide human-readable text within the tags.

For instance, the word "pecan" can be pronounced two different ways. In the following example, the word "pecan" is assigned a different custom pronunciation in each line. Amazon Polly thus uses the pronunciation provided in the `ph` attributes instead of the default pronunciation:

```
1 <speak>
2     You say, <phoneme alphabet="ipa" ph="pkn">pecan</phoneme>.
3     I say, <phoneme alphabet="ipa" ph="pi.kæn">pecan</phoneme>.
4 </speak>
```

Note
In some cases phonetic symbols may include single or double quotes, which conflict with the quote marks used to mark the strings being spoken. Use a backslash in these cases to mark the symbol so it doesn't conflict with the string marker.
For example, when you use the IPA symbol for primary stress (a single quote mark), you would mark it as \'. The X-SAMPA symbol for an open mid-central unrounded r-colored vowel (**3'**) is marked as **3**\'. The single or double quote string marker is not changed.

The `prosody` tag enables you to control the volume, rate, and pitch of the delivery of the text.

The following values can be used for the `volume` attribute, to modify the volume of the speech:

- `default`: Resets volume to default for current voice.

- `silent`, `x-soft`, `soft`, `medium`, `loud`, `x-loud`: Sets the volume to a predefined value for current voice.

- `+ndB`, `-ndB`: Changes the volume relative to the current volume level. A value of "+0dB" means no change of volume, "+6dB" means approximately twice the current amplitude, "-6dB" means approximately half the current amplitude.

The following values can be used for the `rate` attribute, to modify the rate of speech:

- `x-slow`, `slow`, `medium`, `fast`, `x-fast`: Sets the rate of speech to a predefined value for the current voice.

The following values can be used for the `pitch` attribute, to modify the pitch of the voice:

- `default`: Resets pitch to the default pitch for the current voice.

- `x-low`, `low`, `medium`, `high`, `x-high`: Sets the pitch to a predefined value for the current voice.

- `+n%` or `-n%`: Adjusts pitch by a relative percentage change in the current pitch level of the current voice. For example, `+4%`, or `-2%`.

For example, prosody for a passage could be set in the following ways:

```
1 <speak>
2     Prosody can be used to change the way words sound. The following words are
3     <prosody volume="x-loud"> quite a bit louder than the rest of this passage.
4     </prosody> Each morning when I wake up, <prosody rate="x-slow">I speak
5     quite slowly and deliberately until I have my coffee.</prosody> I can also
6     change the pitch of my voice using prosody. Do you like <prosody pitch="+5%">
7     speech with a pitch that is higher,</prosody> or <prosody pitch="-10%">
8     is a lower pitch preferable?</prosody>
9 </speak>
```

This tag indicates a sentence in the text. This is equivalent to:

- Ending a sentence with a period (.).

- Specifying a pause with `<break strength="strong"/>`.

Unlike the `<break strength="strong"/>` tag, this tag needs to enclose the sentence in question.

In this example, the `<s>` tag creates a short pause after both the first and second sentences. The final sentence has no `<s>` tag but also has a short pause after it because it contains a period.

```
1 <speak>
2     <s>Mary had a little lamb</s>
3     <s>Whose fleece was white as snow</s>
4     And everywhere that Mary went, the lamb was sure to go.
5 </speak>
```

\<say-as\>

This tag indicates how the input text should be interpreted. This enables you provide additional context to eliminate any ambiguity on how Amazon Polly should render the text.

When using the `say-as` tag, you need to indicate how Amazon Polly should interpret the text with the `interpret-as` attribute.

The following values are available with the `interpret-as` attribute:

- `character` or `spell-out`: spells out each letter, as in a-b-c.
- `cardinal` or `number`: pronounces the value as a cardinal number, as in 1,234.
- `ordinal`: pronounces the value as an ordinal number, as in 1,234th.
- `digits`: pronounces each digit of the number individually, as in 1-2-3-4.
- `fraction`: pronounces the value as a fraction. This works for both common fractions such as 3/20, and mixed fractions, such as 2 1/2 (see below).
- `unit`: interprets a value as a measurement. The value should be followed by either a number or a fraction followed by a unit (with no space in between), or by just a unit, as in `1meter`.
- `date`: interprets the value as a date. The format of the date must be specified with the format attribute (see below).
- `time`: interprets the value as duration in minutes and seconds, as in `1'21"`.
- `address`: interprets the value as part of a street address.
- `expletive`: "bleeps" out the content included within the tag.
- `telephone`: interprets the value as a 7-digit or 10-digit telephone, as in 2025551212 This can also handle telephone extensions, as in 2025551212x345.

The Amazon Polly service attempts to interpret the text you provide correctly based on the text's formatting even without the `<say-as>` tag. For example, if your text includes "202-555-1212", Amazon Polly will interpret it as a 10-digit telephone number and say each individual digit individually, with a brief pause for each dash. It isn't necessary to use `<say-as interpret-as="telephone">` in this case. However, if you provide the text "2025551212" and want Amazon Polly to say it as a phone number, you need to use `<say-as interpret-as="telephone">`.

The logic underlying the interpretation of each element is language-specific. For example, US and UK English differ in how phone numbers are pronounced (in UK English, sequences of the same digit are grouped together, e.g. "double five" or "triple four"). You can test the following example with a US voice and with a UK voice to demonstrate the difference:

```
1  <speak>
2      Richard's number is <say-as interpret-as="telephone">2122241555</say-as>
3  </speak>
```

Fractions

Amazon Polly will interpret values within the `say-as` having the `interpret-as="fraction"` attribute as common fractions. The following is the syntax for fractions:

- *Fraction*

  Syntax: *cardinal number/cardinal number* such as 2/9.

  For example: `<say-as interpret-as="fraction">2/9</say-as>` is pronounced "two ninths".

- *Non-negative Mixed Number*

  Syntax: *cardinal number+cardinal number/cardinal number* such as 3 1/2.

  For example: `<say-as interpret-as="fraction">3+1/2</say-as>` is pronounced "three and a half".

Dates

The following values can be used when `interpret-as` is set to `date` to indicate the format of the date:

- `mdy`: month-day-year.

- `dmy`: day-month-year.

- `ymd`: year-month-day.

- `md`: month-day.

- `dm`: day-month.

- `ym`: year-month.

- `my`: month-year.

- `d`: day.

- `m`: month.

- `y`: year.

- `yyyymmdd`: year-month-day. If this format is used, you can include question marks for portions of the date to leave out. For instance, `<say-as interpret-as="date">????0922</say-as>` would be "September 22nd."

This tag substitutes the pronunciation inside the `alias` attribute for the pronunciation of the text enclosed in the tag. A common use for this tag is to provide expanded pronunciation for acronyms and abbreviations.

```
1  <speak>
2      My favorite chemical element is <sub alias="mercury">Hg</sub>, it looks cool.
3  </speak>
```

Similar to `<say-as>`, this tag customizes word pronunciation by specifying the word's part of speech. The attribute `role` is included with the tag to specify the part of speech indicated.

The following values can be used for the `role` attribute:

- `amazon:VB`: interprets the word as a verb (present simple).

- `amazon:VBD`: interprets the word as past tense or as a past participle.

- `amazon:SENSE_1`: uses the non-default sense of the word when present. For example, the default meaning of "bass" is that of the low note in a chord or the lowest part of the musical range. This is pronounced differently than the alternate sense a freshwater fish, also called a "bass" but pronounced differently. Using `<w role="amazon:SENSE_1">bass</w>` renders the non-default pronunciation (freshwater fish) for the audio text.

Depending how you intend to use it, the American English pronunciation of the word "read," depending on how it's being used:

```
1 <speak>
2     The present simple form of the word is pronounced <w role="amazon:VB">read</w>,
3 where the past tense or past participle is pronounced <w role="amazon:VBD">read</w>.
4 </speak>
```

<amazon:effect name="drc">

Depending on the text, language, and voice used in an audio file, the sounds range from soft to loud. Environmental sounds, such as the sound of a moving vehicle, can often mask the softer sounds, which makes the audio track difficult to hear clearly. To enhance the volume of certain sounds in your audio file, use the dynamic range compression (`drc`) tag.

The `drc` tag sets a mid-range "loudness" threshold for your audio, and increases the volume (the gain) of the sounds around that threshold. It applies the greatest gain increase closest to the threshold, and the gain increase is lessened farther away from the threshold.

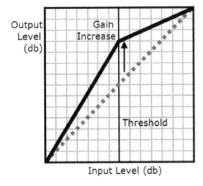

This makes the middle-range sounds easier to hear in a noisy environment, which makes the entire audio file clearer.

The `drc` tag is a Boolean parameter (it's either present or it isn't). It uses the syntax: `<amazon:effect name="drc">` and is closed with `</amazon:effect>`.

You can use the `drc` tag with any voice or language supported by Amazon Polly. You can apply it to an entire section of the recording, or for only a few words. For example:

```
1 <speak>
2     Some audio is difficult to hear in a moving vehicle, but <amazon:effect name="drc"> this
          audio
3     is less difficult to hear in a moving vehicle.</amazon:effect>
4 </speak>
```

Note
When you use "drc" in the amazon:effect syntax, it is case-sensitive.

Using drc with the prosody volume tag
As the following graphic shows, the `prosody volume` tag evenly increases the volume of an entire audio file from the original level (dotted line) to an adjusted level (solid line). To further increase the volume of certain parts of the file, use the `drc` tag with the `prosody volume` tag. Combining tags doesn't affect the settings of the `prosody volume` tag.

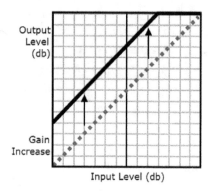

When you use the drc and prosody volume tags together, Amazon Polly applies the drc tag first, increasing the middle-range sounds (those near the threshold). It then applies the prosody volume tag and further increases the volume of the entire audio track evenly.

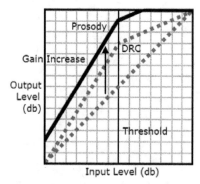

To use the tags together, nest one inside the other. For example:

```
1 <speak>
2     <prosody volume="loud">This text needs to be understandable and loud. <amazon:effect name="
          drc">
3     This text also needs to be more understandable in a moving car.</amazon:effect></prosody>
4 </speak>
```

In this text, the prosody volume tag increases the volume of the entire passage to "loud." The drc tag enhances the volume of the middle-range values in the second sentence.

Note
When using the drc and prosody volume tags together, use standard XML practices for nesting tags.

<amazon:effect phonation="soft">

This tag indicates that the input text should be spoken in a softer than normal voice rather than as normal speech. This can be used with any of the voices in the Amazon Polly Text-to-Speech portfolio. It uses the syntax: <amazon:effect phonation=soft> and is closed with </amazon:effect>.

For example, when using the Matthew voice:

```
1 <speak>
2     This is Matthew speaking in my normal voice. <amazon:effect phonation="soft">This
3     is Matthew speaking in my softer voice.</amazon:effect>
4 </speak>
```

In this case, the first portion of the synthesized speech is spoken with a normal voice, whereas the portion using the phonation tag is spoken more softly.

<amazon:effect vocal-tract-length>

Timbre is the tonal quality of a voice that helps you tell the difference between voices, even when they have the same pitch and loudness. One of the most important physiological features which contribute towards speech timbre is the length of the vocal tract, a cavity of air which spans from the top of the vocal folds up to the edge of the lips.

To control the timbre of output speech in Amazon Polly, use the `vocal-tract-length` tag. This tag has the effect of changing the length of the speaker's vocal tract, which sounds like a change in the speaker's size. When you increase the `vocal-tract-length`, the speaker sounds physically bigger. When you decrease it, the speaker sounds smaller. You can use this tag with any of the voices in the Amazon Polly Text-to-Speech portfolio.

To change timbre, use the following values:

- `+n%` or `-n%`: Adjusts the vocal tract length by a relative percentage change in the current voice. For example, +4% or -2%. Valid values range from +100% to -50%. Values outside this range areclipped. For example, +111% sounds like +100% and -60% sounds like -50%.

- `n%`: Changes the vocal tract length to an absolute percentage of the tract length of the current voice. For example, 110% or 75%. An absolute value of 110% is equivalent to a relative value of +10%. An absolute value of 100% is the same as the default value for the current voice.

The following example shows how to change the vocal tract length to change timbre:

```
1 <speak>
2     This is my original voice, without any modifications. <amazon:effect vocal-tract-length
          ="+15%">
3     Now, imagine that I am much bigger. </amazon:effect> <amazon:effect vocal-tract-length
          ="-15%">
4     Or, perhaps you prefer my voice when I'm very small. </amazon:effect> You can also control
          the
5     timbre of my voice by making minor adjustments. <amazon:effect vocal-tract-length="+10%">
6     For example, by making me sound just a little bigger. </amazon:effect><amazon:effect
7     vocal-tract-length="-10%"> Or, making me sound only somewhat smaller. </amazon:effect>
8 </speak>
```

Combining Multiple Tags

You can combine the `vocal-tract-length` tag with any other SSML tag that is supported by Amazon Polly. Because timbre (vocal tract length) and pitch are closely connected, you might get the best results by using both the `vocal-tract-length` and the `<prosody pitch>` tags". To produce the most realistic voice, you will likely use different percentages of change for the two tags. Experiment with various combinations to get the results you want.

The following example shows how to combine tags.

```
1 <speak>
2     The pitch and timbre of a person's voice are connected in human speech.
3     <amazon:effect vocal-tract-length="-15%"> If you are going to reduce the vocal tract length
          ,
4     </amazon:effect><amazon:effect vocal-tract-length="-15%"> <prosody pitch="+20%"> you
5     might consider increasing the pitch, too. </prosody></amazon:effect>
6     <amazon:effect vocal-tract-length="+15%"> If you choose to lengthen the vocal tract,
7     </amazon:effect> <amazon:effect vocal-tract-length="+15%"> <prosody pitch="-10%">
8     you might also want to lower the pitch. </prosody></amazon:effect>
9 </speak>
```

<amazon:effect name="whispered">

This tag indicates that the input text should be spoken in a whispered voice rather than as normal speech. This can be used with any of the voices in the Amazon Polly Text-to-Speech portfolio. It uses the syntax: `<amazon:effect name=whispered>` and is closed with `</amazon:effect>`.

For example:

```
1  <speak>
2      <amazon:effect name="whispered">If you make any noise, </amazon:effect>
3      she said, <amazon:effect name="whispered">they will hear us.</amazon:effect>
4  </speak>
```

In this case, the synthesized speech spoken by the character will be whispered, whereas the phrase "she said" will be in the normal synthesized speech of the selected Amazon Polly voice.

You can enhance the "whispered" effect by slowing down the prosody rate by up to 10%, depending on the effect you desire.

For example:

```
1  <speak>
2      When any voice is made to whisper, <amazon:effect name="whispered">
3      <prosody rate="-10%">the sound is slower and quieter than normal speech
4      </prosody></amazon:effect>
5  </speak>
```

When generating speech marks for a whispered voice, the audio stream must also include the whispered voice to ensure that the speech marks match the audio stream.

Phonetic Tables Used by Amazon Polly

The following provides a phonetic pronunciation (the phonemes) for Amazon Polly SSML tags for American English.

IPA	X-SAMPA	Description	Example
Consonants			
b	b	Voiced bilabial plosive	bed
d	d	Voiced alveolar plosive	dig
d	dZ	Voiced postalveolar affricate	jump
ð	D	Voiced dental fricative	then
f	f	Voiceless labiodental fricative	five
g	g	Voiced velar plosive	game
h	h	Voiceless glottal fricative	house
j	j	Palatal approximant	yes
k	k	Voiceless velar plosive	cat
l	l	Alveolar lateral approximant	lay
m	m	Bilabial nasal	mouse
n	n	Alveolar nasal	nap
ŋ	N	Velar nasal	thing
p	p	Voiceless bilabial plosive	speak
	r\	Alveolar approximant	red
s	s	Voiceless alveolar fricative	seem
	S	Voiceless postalveolar fricative	ship
t	t	Voiceless alveolar plosive	trap
t	tS	Voiceless postalveolar affricate	chart
Θ	T	Voiceless dental fricative	thin
v	v	Voiced labiodental fricative	vest
w	w	Labial-velar approximant	west
z	z	Voiced alveolar fricative	zero
	Z	Voiced postalveolar fricative	vision
Vowels			
ə	@	Mid central vowel	arena
	@'	Mid central r-colored vowel	reader
æ	{	Near open-front unrounded vowel	trap
a	aI	Diphthong	price
a	aU	Diphthong	mouth

IPA	X-SAMPA	Description	Example
	A	Long open-back unrounded vowel	father
e	eI	Diphthong	face
	3'	Open mid-central unrounded r-colored vowel	nurse
	E	Open mid-front unrounded vowel	dress
i:	i	Long close front unrounded vowel	fleece
	I	Near-close near-front unrounded vowel	kit
o	oU	Diphthong	goat
	O	Long open mid-back rounded vowel	thought
	OI	Diphthong	choice
u	u	Long close-back rounded vowel	goose
	U	Near-close near-back rounded vowel	foot
	V	Open-mid-back unrounded vowel	strut
Other Symbols			
'	"	primary stress	Alabama
ˌ	%	secondary stress	Alabama
.	.	syllable boundary	A.la.ba.ma

Managing Lexicons

Pronunciation lexicons enable you to customize the pronunciation of words. Amazon Polly provides API operations that you can use to store lexicons in an AWS region. Those lexicons are then specific to that particular region. You can use one or more of the lexicons from that region when synthesizing the text by using the `SynthesizeSpeech` operation. This applies the specified lexicon to the input text before the synthesis begins. For more information, see SynthesizeSpeech.

Note

These lexicons must conform with the Pronunciation Lexicon Specification (PLS) W3C recommendation. For more information, see Pronunciation Lexicon Specification (PLS) Version 1.0 on the W3C website.

The following are examples of ways to use lexicons with speech synthesis engines:

- Common words are sometimes stylized with numbers taking the place of letters, as with "g3t sm4rt" (get smart). Humans can read these words correctly. However, a Text-to-Speech (TTS) engine reads the text literally, pronouncing the name exactly as it is spelled. This is where you can leverage lexicons to customize the synthesized speech by using Amazon Polly. In this example, you can specify an alias (get smart) for the word "g3t sm4rt" in the lexicon.

- Your text might include an acronym, such as W3C. You can use a lexicon to define an alias for the word W3C so that it is read in the full, expanded form (World Wide Web Consortium).

Lexicons give you additional control over how Amazon Polly pronounces words uncommon to the selected language. For example, you can specify the pronunciation using a phonetic alphabet. For more information, see Pronunciation Lexicon Specification (PLS) Version 1.0 on the W3C website.

- Applying Multiple Lexicons
- Managing Lexicons Using the Amazon Polly Console
- Managing Lexicons Using the AWS CLI

Applying Multiple Lexicons

You can apply up to five lexicons to your text. If the same grapheme appears in more than one lexicon that you apply to your text, the order in which they are applied can make a difference in the resulting speech. For example, given the following text, "Hello, my name is Bob." and two lexemes in different lexicons that both use the grapheme Bob.

LexA

```
1 <lexeme>
2     <grapheme>Bob</grapheme>
3     <alias>Robert</alias>
4 </lexeme>
```

LexB

```
1 <lexeme>
2     <grapheme>Bob</grapheme>
3     <alias>Bobby</alias>
4 </lexeme>
```

If the lexicons are listed in the order LexA and then LexB, the synthesized speech will be "Hello, my name is Robert." If they are listed in the order LexB and then LexA, the synthesized speech is "Hello, my name is Bobby."

Example – Applying LexA Before LexB

```
1 aws polly synthesize-speech \
2 --lexicon-names LexA LexB \
3 --output-format mp3 \
4 --text 'Hello, my name is Bob' \
5 --voice-id Justin \
6 bobAB.mp3
```

Speech output: "Hello, my name is Robert."

Example – Applying LexB before LexA

```
1 aws polly synthesize-speech \
2 --lexicon-names LexB LexA \
3 --output-format mp3 \
4 --text 'Hello, my name is Bob' \
5 --voice-id Justin \
6 bobBA.mp3
```

Speech output: "Hello, my name is Bobby."

For information about applying lexicons using the Amazon Polly console, see Applying Lexicons Using the Console (Synthesize Speech).

Managing Lexicons Using the Amazon Polly Console

You can use the Amazon Polly console to upload, download, apply, filter, and delete lexicons. The following procedures demonstrate each of these processes.

Uploading Lexicons Using the Console

To use a pronunciation lexicon, you must first upload it. There are two locations on the console from which you can upload a lexicon, the **Text-to-Speech** tab and the **Lexicons** tab.

The following processes describe how to add lexicons that you can use to customize how words and phrases uncommon to the chosen language are pronounced.

To add a lexicon from the Lexicons Tab

1. Sign in to the AWS Management Console and open the Amazon Polly console at https://console.aws. amazon.com/polly/.

2. Choose the **Lexicons** tab.

3. Choose **Upload**.

4. Browse to find the lexicon that you want to upload. You can use only PLS files that use the .pls and .xml extensions.

5. Choose **Open**. If a lexicon by the same name (whether a .pls or .xml file) already exists, uploading the lexicon will overwrite the existing lexicon.

To add a lexicon from the Text-to-Speech Tab

1. Sign in to the AWS Management Console and open the Amazon Polly console at https://console.aws. amazon.com/polly/.

2. Choose the **Text-to-Speech** tab.

3. Choose **Customize pronunciation of words or phrases using lexicons**, then choose **Upload lexicon**.

4. Browse to find the lexicon that you want to upload. You can use only PLS files that use the .pls and .xml extensions.

5. Choose **Open**. If a lexicon with the same name (whether a .pls or .xml file) already exists, uploading the lexicon will overwrite the existing lexicon.

Applying Lexicons Using the Console (Synthesize Speech)

The following procedure demonstrates how to apply a lexicon to your input text by applying the `W3c.pls` lexicon to substitute "World Wide Web Consortium" for "W3C". If you apply multiple lexicons to your text they are applied in a top-down order with the first match taking precedence over later matches. A lexicon is applied to the text only if the language specified in the lexicon is the same as the language chosen.

You can apply a lexicon to plain text or SSML input.

Example – Applying the W3C.pls Lexicon
To create the lexicon you'll need for this exercise, see Using the PutLexicon Operation. Use a plain text editor to create the W3C.pls lexicon shown at the top of the topic. Remember where you save this file.

To apply the W3C.pls lexicon to your input

In this example we introduce a lexicon to substitute "World Wide Web Consortium" for "W3C". Compare the results of this exercise with that of Using SSML with the Amazon Polly Console for both US English and another language.

1. Sign in to the AWS Management Console and open the Amazon Polly console at https://console.aws.amazon.com/polly/.

2. Do one of the following:

   - Choose the **Plain text** tab and then type or paste this text into the text input box.

   ```
   1 He was caught up in the game.
   2 In the middle of the 10/3/2014 W3C meeting
   3 he shouted, "Score!" quite loudly.
   ```

   - Choose the **SSML** tab and then type or paste this text into the text input box.

   ```
   1 <speak>He wasn't paying attention.<break time="1s"/>
   2 In the middle of the 10/3/2014 W3C meeting
   3 he shouted, "Score!" quite loudly.</speak>
   ```

3. From the **Choose a language and region** list, choose English US, then choose a voice you want to use for this text.

4. Choose **Customize pronunciation of words or phrases using lexicons**.

5. From the list of lexicons, choose W3C (English, US).

   If the W3C (English, US) lexicon is not listed, choose **Upload lexicon** and upload it, then choose it from the list. To create this lexicon, see Using the PutLexicon Operation.

6. To listen to the speech immediately, choose **Listen to speech**.

7. To save the speech to a file,

   1. Choose **Save speech to MP3**.

   2. To change to a different file format, choose **Change file format**, choose the file format you want, and then choose **Change**. Repeat the previous steps, but choose a different language and notice the difference in the output.

Filtering the Lexicon List Using the Console

The following procedure describes how to filter the lexicons list so that only lexicons of a chosen language are displayed.

To filter the lexicons listed by language

1. Sign in to the AWS Management Console and open the Amazon Polly console at https://console.aws.amazon.com/polly/.

2. Choose the **Lexicons** tab.

3. Choose **Filter**.

4. From the list of languages, choose the language you want to filter on.

   The list displays only the lexicons for the chosen language.

Downloading Lexicons Using the Console

The following process describes how to download one or more lexicons. You can add, remove, or modify lexicon entries in the file and then upload it again to keep your lexicon up-to-date.

To download one or more lexicons

1. Sign in to the AWS Management Console and open the Amazon Polly console at https://console.aws. amazon.com/polly/.

2. Choose the **Lexicons** tab.

3. Choose the lexicon or lexicons you want to download.

    1. To download a single lexicon, choose its name from the list.

    2. To download multiple lexicons as a single compressed archive file, select the check box next to each entry in the list that you want to download.

4. Choose **Download**.

5. Open the folder where you want to download the lexicon.

6. Choose **Save**.

Deleting a Lexicon Using the Console

To delete a lexicon

The following process describes how to delete a lexicon. After deleting the lexicon, you must add it back before you can use it again. You can delete one or more lexicons at the same time by selecting the check boxes next to individual lexicons.

1. Sign in to the AWS Management Console and open the Amazon Polly console at https://console.aws. amazon.com/polly/.

2. Choose the **Lexicons** tab.

3. Choose one or more lexicons that you want to delete from the list.

4. Choose **Delete**.

5. Choose **Delete** to remove the lexicon from the region or **Cancel** to keep it.

Managing Lexicons Using the AWS CLI

The following topics cover the AWS CLI commands needed to manage your pronunciation lexicons.

- Using the PutLexicon Operation
- Using the GetLexicon Operation
- Using the ListLexicons Operations
- Using the DeleteLexicon Operation

Using the PutLexicon Operation

With Amazon Polly, you can use PutLexicon to store pronunciation lexicons in a specific AWS Region for your account. Then, you can specify one or more of these stored lexicons in your SynthesizeSpeech request that you want to apply before the service starts synthesizing the text. For more information, see Managing Lexicons.

This section provides example lexicons and step-by-step instructions for storing and testing them.

Note
These lexicons must conform to the Pronunciation Lexicon Specification (PLS) W3C recommendation. For more information, see Pronunciation Lexicon Specification (PLS) Version 1.0 on the W3C website.

Example 1: Lexicon with One Lexeme

Consider the following W3C PLS-compliant lexicon.

```
1  <?xml version="1.0" encoding="UTF-8"?>
2  <lexicon version="1.0"
3        xmlns="http://www.w3.org/2005/01/pronunciation-lexicon"
4        xmlns:xsi="http://www.w3.org/2001/XMLSchema-instance"
5        xsi:schemaLocation="http://www.w3.org/2005/01/pronunciation-lexicon
6          http://www.w3.org/TR/2007/CR-pronunciation-lexicon-20071212/pls.xsd"
7        alphabet="ipa"
8        xml:lang="en-US">
9    <lexeme>
10     <grapheme>W3C</grapheme>
11     <alias>World Wide Web Consortium</alias>
12   </lexeme>
13 </lexicon>
```

Note the following:

- The two attributes specified in the `<lexicon>` element:

    - The `xml:lang` attribute specifies the language code, en-US, to which the lexicon applies. Amazon Polly can use this example lexicon if the voice you specify in the **SynthesizeSpeech** call has the same language code (en-US). **Note**
    You can use the **DescribeVoices** operation to find the language code associated with a voice.

    - The `alphabet` attribute specifies IPA, which means that the International Phonetic Alphabet (IPA) alphabet is used for pronunciations. IPA is one of the alphabets for writing pronunciations. Amazon Polly also supports the Extended Speech Assessment Methods Phonetic Alphabet (X-SAMPA).

- The `<lexeme>` element describes the mapping between `<grapheme>` (that is, a textual representation of the word) and `<alias>`.

To test this lexicon, do the following:

1. Save the lexicon as `example.pls`.

2. Run the `put-lexicon` AWS CLI command to store the lexicon (with the name w3c), in the us-east-2 region.

```
1  aws polly put-lexicon \
2  --name w3c \
3  --content file://example.pls
```

3. Run the `synthesize-speech` command to synthesize sample text to an audio stream (`speech.mp3`), and specify the optional `lexicon-name` parameter.

```
1 aws polly synthesize-speech \
2 --text 'W3C is a Consortium' \
3 --voice-id Joanna \
4 --output-format mp3 \
5 --lexicon-names="w3c" \
6 speech.mp3
```

4. Play the resulting `speech.mp3`, and notice that the word W3C in the text is replaced by World Wide Web Consortium.

The preceding example lexicon uses an alias. The IPA alphabet mentioned in the lexicon is not used. The following lexicon specifies a phonetic pronunciation using the `<phoneme>` element with the IPA alphabet.

```
1 <?xml version="1.0" encoding="UTF-8"?>
2 <lexicon version="1.0"
3      xmlns="http://www.w3.org/2005/01/pronunciation-lexicon"
4      xmlns:xsi="http://www.w3.org/2001/XMLSchema-instance"
5      xsi:schemaLocation="http://www.w3.org/2005/01/pronunciation-lexicon
6        http://www.w3.org/TR/2007/CR-pronunciation-lexicon-20071212/pls.xsd"
7      alphabet="ipa"
8      xml:lang="en-US">
9   <lexeme>
10     <grapheme>pecan</grapheme>
11     <phoneme>pkn</phoneme>
12   </lexeme>
13 </lexicon>
```

Follow the same steps to test this lexicon. Make sure you specify input text that has word "pecan" (for example, "Pecan pie is delicious").

Example 2: Lexicon with Multiple Lexemes

In this example, the lexeme that you specify in the lexicon applies exclusively to the input text for the synthesis. Consider the following lexicon:

```
1 <?xml version="1.0" encoding="UTF-8"?>
2 <lexicon version="1.0"
3      xmlns="http://www.w3.org/2005/01/pronunciation-lexicon"
4      xmlns:xsi="http://www.w3.org/2001/XMLSchema-instance"
5      xsi:schemaLocation="http://www.w3.org/2005/01/pronunciation-lexicon
6        http://www.w3.org/TR/2007/CR-pronunciation-lexicon-20071212/pls.xsd"
7      alphabet="ipa" xml:lang="en-US">
8
9   <lexeme>
10     <grapheme>W3C</grapheme>
11     <alias>World Wide Web Consortium</alias>
12   </lexeme>
13   <lexeme>
14     <grapheme>W3C</grapheme>
15     <alias>WWW Consortium</alias>
16   </lexeme>
17   <lexeme>
18     <grapheme>Consortium</grapheme>
```

```
19      <alias>Community</alias>
20    </lexeme>
21  </lexicon>
```

The lexicon specifies three lexemes, two of which define an alias for the grapheme W3C as follows:

- The first `<lexeme>` element defines an alias (World Wide Web Consortium).

- The second `<lexeme>` defines an alternative alias (WWW Consortium).

Amazon Polly uses the first replacement for any given grapheme in a lexicon.

The third `<lexeme>` defines a replacement (Community) for the word Consortium.

First, let's test this lexicon. Suppose you want to synthesize the following sample text to an audio file (`speech.mp3`), and you specify the lexicon in a call to SynthesizeSpeech.

```
1 The W3C is a Consortium
```

SynthesizeSpeech first applies the lexicon as follows:

- As per the first lexeme, the word W3C is revised as World Wide Web Consortium. The revised text appears as follows:

```
1 The World Wide Web Consortium is a Consortium
```

- The alias defined in the third lexeme applies only to the word Consortium that was part of the original text, resulting in the following text:

```
1 The World Wide Web Consortium is a Community.
```

You can test this using the AWS CLI as follows:

1. Save the lexicon as `example.pls`.

2. Run the `put-lexicon` command to store the lexicon with name w3c in the us-east-2 region.

```
1 aws polly put-lexicon \
2 --name w3c \
3 --content file://example.pls
```

3. Run the `list-lexicons` command to verify that the w3c lexicon is in the list of lexicons returned.

```
1 aws polly list-lexicons
```

4. Run the `synthesize-speech` command to synthesize sample text to an audio file (`speech.mp3`), and specify the optional `lexicon-name` parameter.

```
1 aws polly synthesize-speech \
2 --text 'W3C is a Consortium' \
3 --voice-id Joanna \
4 --output-format mp3 \
5 --lexicon-names="w3c" \
6 speech.mp3
```

5. Play the resulting `speech.mp3` file to verify that the synthesized speech reflects the text changes.

Example 3: Specifying Multiple Lexicons

In a call to SynthesizeSpeech, you can specify multiple lexicons. In this case, the first lexicon specified (in order from left to right) overrides any preceding lexicons.

Consider the following two lexicons. Note that each lexicon describes different aliases for the same grapheme W3C.

- Lexicon 1: w3c.pls

```
1  <?xml version="1.0" encoding="UTF-8"?>
2  <lexicon version="1.0"
3      xmlns="http://www.w3.org/2005/01/pronunciation-lexicon"
4      xmlns:xsi="http://www.w3.org/2001/XMLSchema-instance"
5      xsi:schemaLocation="http://www.w3.org/2005/01/pronunciation-lexicon
6        http://www.w3.org/TR/2007/CR-pronunciation-lexicon-20071212/pls.xsd"
7      alphabet="ipa" xml:lang="en-US">
8    <lexeme>
9      <grapheme>W3C</grapheme>
10     <alias>World Wide Web Consortium</alias>
11   </lexeme>
12 </lexicon>
```

- Lexicon 2: w3cAlternate.pls

```
1  <?xml version="1.0" encoding="UTF-8"?>
2  <lexicon version="1.0"
3      xmlns="http://www.w3.org/2005/01/pronunciation-lexicon"
4      xmlns:xsi="http://www.w3.org/2001/XMLSchema-instance"
5      xsi:schemaLocation="http://www.w3.org/2005/01/pronunciation-lexicon
6        http://www.w3.org/TR/2007/CR-pronunciation-lexicon-20071212/pls.xsd"
7      alphabet="ipa" xml:lang="en-US">
8
9    <lexeme>
10     <grapheme>W3C</grapheme>
11     <alias>WWW Consortium</alias>
12   </lexeme>
13 </lexicon>
```

Suppose you store these lexicons as w3c and w3cAlternate respectively. If you specify lexicons in order (w3c followed by w3cAlternate) in a SynthesizeSpeech call, the alias for W3C defined in the first lexicon has precedence over the second. To test the lexicons, do the following:

1. Save the lexicons locally in files called w3c.pls and w3cAlternate.pls.

2. Upload these lexicons using the put-lexicon AWS CLI command.

   - Upload the w3c.pls lexicon and store it as w3c.

   ```
   1 aws polly put-lexicon \
   2 --name w3c \
   3 --content file://w3c.pls
   ```

   - Upload thew3cAlternate.pls lexicon on the service as w3cAlternate.

   ```
   1 aws polly put-lexicon \
   2 --name w3cAlternate \
   3 --content file://w3cAlternate.pls
   ```

3. Run the `synthesize-speech` command to synthesize sample text to an audio stream (`speech.mp3`), and specify both lexicons using the `lexicon-name` parameter.

```
1 aws polly synthesize-speech \
2 --text 'PLS is a W3C recommendation' \
3 --voice-id Joanna \
4 --output-format mp3 \
5 --lexicon-names '["w3c","w3cAlternative"]' \
6 speech.mp3
```

4. Test the resulting `speech.mp3`. It should read as follows:

```
1 PLS is a World Wide Web Consortium recommendation
```

Additional Code Samples for the PutLexicon API

- Java Sample: PutLexicon
- Python (Boto3) Sample: PutLexicon

Using the GetLexicon Operation

Amazon Polly provides the GetLexicon API operation to retrieve the content of a pronunciation lexicon you stored in your account in a specific region.

The following `get-lexicon` AWS CLI command retrieves the content of the `example` lexicon.

```
1  aws polly get-lexicon \
2  --name example
```

If you don't already have a lexicon stored in your account, you can use the `PutLexicon` operation to store one. For more information, see Using the PutLexicon Operation.

The following is a sample response. In addition to the lexicon content, the response returns the metadata, such as the language code to which the lexicon applies, number of lexemes defined in the lexicon, the Amazon Resource Name (ARN) of the resource, and the size of the lexicon in bytes. The `LastModified` value is a Unix timestamp.

```
1  {
2      "Lexicon": {
3          "Content": "lexicon content in plain text PLS format",
4          "Name": "example"
5      },
6      "LexiconAttributes": {
7          "LanguageCode": "en-US",
8          "LastModified": 1474222543.989,
9          "Alphabet": "ipa",
10         "LexemesCount": 1,
11         "LexiconArn": "arn:aws:polly:us-east-2:account-id:lexicon/example",
12         "Size": 495
13     }
14 }
```

Additional Code Samples for the GetLexicon API

- Java Sample: GetLexicon
- Python (Boto3) Sample: GetLexicon

Using the ListLexicons Operations

Amazon Polly provides the ListLexicons API operation that you can use to get the list of pronunciation lexicons in your account in a specific AWS Region. The following AWS CLI call lists the lexicons in your account in the us-east-2 region.

```
1 aws polly list-lexicons
```

The following is an example response, showing two lexicons named w3c and tomato. For each lexicon, the response returns metadata such as the language code to which the lexicon applies, the number of lexemes defined in the lexicon, the size in bytes, and so on. The language code describes a language and locale to which the lexemes defined in the lexicon apply.

```
1  {
2      "Lexicons": [
3          {
4              "Attributes": {
5                  "LanguageCode": "en-US",
6                  "LastModified": 1474222543.989,
7                  "Alphabet": "ipa",
8                  "LexemesCount": 1,
9                  "LexiconArn": "arn:aws:polly:aws-region:account-id:lexicon/w3c",
10                 "Size": 495
11             },
12             "Name": "w3c"
13         },
14         {
15             "Attributes": {
16                 "LanguageCode": "en-US",
17                 "LastModified": 1473099290.858,
18                 "Alphabet": "ipa",
19                 "LexemesCount": 1,
20                 "LexiconArn": "arn:aws:polly:aws-region:account-id:lexicon/tomato",
21                 "Size": 645
22             },
23             "Name": "tomato"
24         }
25     ]
26 }
```

Additional Code Samples for the ListLexicon API

- Java Sample: ListLexicons
- Python (Boto3) Sample: ListLexicon

Using the DeleteLexicon Operation

Amazon Polly provides the DeleteLexicon API operation to delete a pronunciation lexicon from a specific AWS Region in your account. The following AWS CLI deletes the specified lexicon.

The following AWS CLI example is formatted for Unix, Linux, and macOS. For Windows, replace the backslash (\) Unix continuation character at the end of each line with a caret (^) and use full quotation marks (") around the input text with single quotes (') for interior tags.

```
1 aws polly delete-lexicon \
2 --name example
```

Additional Code Samples for the DeleteLexicon API

- Java Sample: DeleteLexicon
- Python (Boto3) Sample: DeleteLexicon

Code and Application Examples

This section provides code samples and example applications that you can use to explore Amazon Polly.

- Sample Code
- Example Applications

The **Sample Code** topic contains snippets of code organized by programming language and separated into examples for different Amazon Polly functionality. The **Example Application** topic contains applications organized by programming language that can be used independently to explore Amazon Polly.

Before you start using these examples, we recommend that you first read Amazon Polly: How It Works and follow the steps described in Getting Started with Amazon Polly.

Sample Code

This topic contains code samples for various functionality which can be used to explore Amazon Polly.

- Java Samples
- Python Samples

Java Samples

The following code samples show how to use Java-based applications to accomplish various tasks with Amazon Polly. These samples are not full examples, but can be included in larger Java applications that use the AWS SDK for Java.

- DeleteLexicon
- DescribeVoices
- GetLexicon
- ListLexicons
- PutLexicon
- Speech Marks
- SynthesizeSpeech

DeleteLexicon

Deletes the specified pronunciation lexicon stored in an AWS Region. A lexicon which has been deleted is not available for speech synthesis, nor is it possible to retrieve it using either the `GetLexicon` or `ListLexicon` APIs.

For more information, see Managing Lexicons.

Request Syntax

```
1 DELETE /v1/lexicons/LexiconName HTTP/1.1
```

URI Request Parameters

The request requires the following URI parameters.

** Name **
The name of the lexicon to delete. Must be an existing lexicon in the region.
Pattern: `[0-9A-Za-z]{1,20}`

Request Body

The request does not have a request body.

Response Syntax

```
1 HTTP/1.1 200
```

Response Elements

If the action is successful, the service sends back an HTTP 200 response with an empty HTTP body.

Errors

LexiconNotFoundException
Amazon Polly can't find the specified lexicon. This could be caused by a lexicon that is missing, its name is misspelled or specifying a lexicon that is in a different region.
Verify that the lexicon exists, is in the region (see ListLexicons) and that you spelled its name is spelled correctly. Then try again.
HTTP Status Code: 404

ServiceFailureException
An unknown condition has caused a service failure.
HTTP Status Code: 500

See Also

For more information about using this API in one of the language-specific AWS SDKs, see the following:

- AWS Command Line Interface
- AWS SDK for .NET

- AWS SDK for C++
- AWS SDK for Go
- AWS SDK for Java
- AWS SDK for JavaScript
- AWS SDK for PHP V3
- AWS SDK for Python
- AWS SDK for Ruby V2

DescribeVoices

Returns the list of voices that are available for use when requesting speech synthesis. Each voice speaks a specified language, is either male or female, and is identified by an ID, which is the ASCII version of the voice name.

When synthesizing speech (SynthesizeSpeech), you provide the voice ID for the voice you want from the list of voices returned by DescribeVoices.

For example, you want your news reader application to read news in a specific language, but giving a user the option to choose the voice. Using the DescribeVoices operation you can provide the user with a list of available voices to select from.

You can optionally specify a language code to filter the available voices. For example, if you specify en-US, the operation returns a list of all available US English voices.

This operation requires permissions to perform the polly:DescribeVoices action.

Request Syntax

```
1 GET /v1/voices?LanguageCode=LanguageCode&NextToken=NextToken HTTP/1.1
```

URI Request Parameters

The request requires the following URI parameters.

** LanguageCode **
The language identification tag (ISO 639 code for the language name-ISO 3166 country code) for filtering the list of voices returned. If you don't specify this optional parameter, all available voices are returned.
Valid Values:cy-GB | da-DK | de-DE | en-AU | en-GB | en-GB-WLS | en-IN | en-US | es-ES | es-US | fr-CA | fr-FR | is-IS | it-IT | ko-KR | ja-JP | nb-NO | nl-NL | pl-PL | pt-BR | pt-PT | ro-RO | ru-RU | sv-SE | tr-TR

** NextToken **
An opaque pagination token returned from the previous DescribeVoices operation. If present, this indicates where to continue the listing.

Request Body

The request does not have a request body.

Response Syntax

```
1 HTTP/1.1 200
2 Content-type: application/json
3
4 {
5     "NextToken": "string",
6     "Voices": [
7         {
8             "Gender": "string",
9             "Id": "string",
10            "LanguageCode": "string",
11            "LanguageName": "string",
```

```
12          "Name": "string"
13      }
14    ]
15 }
```

Response Elements

If the action is successful, the service sends back an HTTP 200 response.

The following data is returned in JSON format by the service.

** NextToken **
The pagination token to use in the next request to continue the listing of voices. `NextToken` is returned only if the response is truncated.
Type: String

** Voices **
A list of voices with their properties.
Type: Array of Voice objects

Errors

InvalidNextTokenException
The NextToken is invalid. Verify that it's spelled correctly, and then try again.
HTTP Status Code: 400

ServiceFailureException
An unknown condition has caused a service failure.
HTTP Status Code: 500

See Also

For more information about using this API in one of the language-specific AWS SDKs, see the following:

- AWS Command Line Interface
- AWS SDK for .NET
- AWS SDK for C++
- AWS SDK for Go
- AWS SDK for Java
- AWS SDK for JavaScript
- AWS SDK for PHP V3
- AWS SDK for Python
- AWS SDK for Ruby V2

GetLexicon

Returns the content of the specified pronunciation lexicon stored in an AWS Region. For more information, see Managing Lexicons.

Request Syntax

```
1 GET /v1/lexicons/LexiconName HTTP/1.1
```

URI Request Parameters

The request requires the following URI parameters.

** Name **
Name of the lexicon.
Pattern: [0-9A-Za-z]{1,20}

Request Body

The request does not have a request body.

Response Syntax

```
1 HTTP/1.1 200
2 Content-type: application/json
3
4 {
5     "Lexicon": {
6         "Content": "string",
7         "Name": "string"
8     },
9     "LexiconAttributes": {
10         "Alphabet": "string",
11         "LanguageCode": "string",
12         "LastModified": number,
13         "LexemesCount": number,
14         "LexiconArn": "string",
15         "Size": number
16     }
17 }
```

Response Elements

If the action is successful, the service sends back an HTTP 200 response.

The following data is returned in JSON format by the service.

** Lexicon **
Lexicon object that provides name and the string content of the lexicon.
Type: Lexicon object

** LexiconAttributes **
Metadata of the lexicon, including phonetic alphabetic used, language code, lexicon ARN, number of lexemes

defined in the lexicon, and size of lexicon in bytes.
Type: LexiconAttributes object

Errors

LexiconNotFoundException
Amazon Polly can't find the specified lexicon. This could be caused by a lexicon that is missing, its name is misspelled or specifying a lexicon that is in a different region.
Verify that the lexicon exists, is in the region (see ListLexicons) and that you spelled its name is spelled correctly. Then try again.
HTTP Status Code: 404

ServiceFailureException
An unknown condition has caused a service failure.
HTTP Status Code: 500

See Also

For more information about using this API in one of the language-specific AWS SDKs, see the following:

- AWS Command Line Interface

- AWS SDK for .NET

- AWS SDK for C++

- AWS SDK for Go

- AWS SDK for Java

- AWS SDK for JavaScript

- AWS SDK for PHP V3

- AWS SDK for Python

- AWS SDK for Ruby V2

ListLexicons

Returns a list of pronunciation lexicons stored in an AWS Region. For more information, see Managing Lexicons.

Request Syntax

```
1 GET /v1/lexicons?NextToken=NextToken HTTP/1.1
```

URI Request Parameters

The request requires the following URI parameters.

** NextToken **
An opaque pagination token returned from previous ListLexicons operation. If present, indicates where to continue the list of lexicons.

Request Body

The request does not have a request body.

Response Syntax

```
1  HTTP/1.1 200
2  Content-type: application/json
3
4  {
5     "Lexicons": [
6        {
7           "Attributes": {
8              "Alphabet": "string",
9              "LanguageCode": "string",
10             "LastModified": number,
11             "LexemesCount": number,
12             "LexiconArn": "string",
13             "Size": number
14          },
15          "Name": "string"
16       }
17    ],
18    "NextToken": "string"
19 }
```

Response Elements

If the action is successful, the service sends back an HTTP 200 response.

The following data is returned in JSON format by the service.

** Lexicons **
A list of lexicon names and attributes.
Type: Array of LexiconDescription objects

** NextToken **
The pagination token to use in the next request to continue the listing of lexicons. `NextToken` is returned only if the response is truncated.
Type: String

Errors

InvalidNextTokenException
The NextToken is invalid. Verify that it's spelled correctly, and then try again.
HTTP Status Code: 400

ServiceFailureException
An unknown condition has caused a service failure.
HTTP Status Code: 500

See Also

For more information about using this API in one of the language-specific AWS SDKs, see the following:

- AWS Command Line Interface
- AWS SDK for .NET
- AWS SDK for C++
- AWS SDK for Go
- AWS SDK for Java
- AWS SDK for JavaScript
- AWS SDK for PHP V3
- AWS SDK for Python
- AWS SDK for Ruby V2

PutLexicon

Stores a pronunciation lexicon in an AWS Region. If a lexicon with the same name already exists in the region, it is overwritten by the new lexicon. Lexicon operations have eventual consistency, therefore, it might take some time before the lexicon is available to the SynthesizeSpeech operation.

For more information, see Managing Lexicons.

Request Syntax

```
1 PUT /v1/lexicons/LexiconName HTTP/1.1
2 Content-type: application/json
3
4 {
5    "Content": "string"
6 }
```

URI Request Parameters

The request requires the following URI parameters.

** Name **
Name of the lexicon. The name must follow the regular express format [0-9A-Za-z]{1,20}. That is, the name is a case-sensitive alphanumeric string up to 20 characters long.
Pattern: `[0-9A-Za-z]{1,20}`

Request Body

The request accepts the following data in JSON format.

** Content **
Content of the PLS lexicon as string data.
Type: String
Required: Yes

Response Syntax

```
1 HTTP/1.1 200
```

Response Elements

If the action is successful, the service sends back an HTTP 200 response with an empty HTTP body.

Errors

InvalidLexiconException
Amazon Polly can't find the specified lexicon. Verify that the lexicon's name is spelled correctly, and then try again.
HTTP Status Code: 400

LexiconSizeExceededException

The maximum size of the specified lexicon would be exceeded by this operation.
HTTP Status Code: 400

MaxLexemeLengthExceededException

The maximum size of the lexeme would be exceeded by this operation.
HTTP Status Code: 400

MaxLexiconsNumberExceededException

The maximum number of lexicons would be exceeded by this operation.
HTTP Status Code: 400

ServiceFailureException

An unknown condition has caused a service failure.
HTTP Status Code: 500

UnsupportedPlsAlphabetException

The alphabet specified by the lexicon is not a supported alphabet. Valid values are `x-sampa` and `ipa`.
HTTP Status Code: 400

UnsupportedPlsLanguageException

The language specified in the lexicon is unsupported. For a list of supported languages, see Lexicon Attributes.
HTTP Status Code: 400

See Also

For more information about using this API in one of the language-specific AWS SDKs, see the following:

- AWS Command Line Interface
- AWS SDK for .NET
- AWS SDK for C++
- AWS SDK for Go
- AWS SDK for Java
- AWS SDK for JavaScript
- AWS SDK for PHP V3
- AWS SDK for Python
- AWS SDK for Ruby V2

SynthesizeSpeech

Synthesizes UTF-8 input, plain text or SSML, to a stream of bytes. SSML input must be valid, well-formed SSML. Some alphabets might not be available with all the voices (for example, Cyrillic might not be read at all by English voices) unless phoneme mapping is used. For more information, see How it Works.

Request Syntax

```
1  POST /v1/speech HTTP/1.1
2  Content-type: application/json
3
4  {
5     "LexiconNames": [ "string" ],
6     "OutputFormat": "string",
7     "SampleRate": "string",
8     "SpeechMarkTypes": [ "string" ],
9     "Text": "string",
10    "TextType": "string",
11    "VoiceId": "string"
12 }
```

URI Request Parameters

The request does not use any URI parameters.

Request Body

The request accepts the following data in JSON format.

** LexiconNames **
List of one or more pronunciation lexicon names you want the service to apply during synthesis. Lexicons are applied only if the language of the lexicon is the same as the language of the voice. For information about storing lexicons, see PutLexicon.
Type: Array of strings
Array Members: Maximum number of 5 items.
Pattern: [0-9A-Za-z]{1,20}
Required: No

** OutputFormat **
The format in which the returned output will be encoded. For audio stream, this will be mp3, ogg_vorbis, or pcm. For speech marks, this will be json.
Type: String
Valid Values: json | mp3 | ogg_vorbis | pcm
Required: Yes

** SampleRate **
The audio frequency specified in Hz.
The valid values for mp3 and ogg_vorbis are "8000", "16000", and "22050". The default value is "22050".
Valid values for pcm are "8000" and "16000" The default value is "16000".
Type: String
Required: No

** SpeechMarkTypes **
The type of speech marks returned for the input text.

Type: Array of strings
Array Members: Maximum number of 4 items.
Valid Values:`sentence | ssml | viseme | word`
Required: No

** Text **
Input text to synthesize. If you specify `ssml` as the `TextType`, follow the SSML format for the input text.
Type: String
Required: Yes

** TextType **
Specifies whether the input text is plain text or SSML. The default value is plain text. For more information, see Using SSML.
Type: String
Valid Values:`ssml | text`
Required: No

** VoiceId **
Voice ID to use for the synthesis. You can get a list of available voice IDs by calling the DescribeVoices operation.
Type: String
Valid Values:`Geraint | Gwyneth | Mads | Naja | Hans | Marlene | Nicole | Russell | Amy | Brian | Emma | Raveena | Ivy | Joanna | Joey | Justin | Kendra | Kimberly | Matthew | Salli | Conchita | Enrique | Miguel | Penelope | Chantal | Celine | Mathieu | Dora | Karl | Carla | Giorgio | Mizuki | Liv | Lotte | Ruben | Ewa | Jacek | Jan | Maja | Ricardo | Vitoria | Cristiano | Ines | Carmen | Maxim | Tatyana | Astrid | Filiz | Vicki | Takumi | Seoyeon | Aditi`
Required: Yes

Response Syntax

```
1 HTTP/1.1 200
2 Content-Type: ContentType
3 x-amzn-RequestCharacters: RequestCharacters
4
5 AudioStream
```

Response Elements

If the action is successful, the service sends back an HTTP 200 response.

The response returns the following HTTP headers.

** ContentType **
Specifies the type audio stream. This should reflect the `OutputFormat` parameter in your request.

- If you request `mp3` as the `OutputFormat`, the `ContentType` returned is audio/mpeg.

- If you request `ogg_vorbis` as the `OutputFormat`, the `ContentType` returned is audio/ogg.

- If you request `pcm` as the `OutputFormat`, the `ContentType` returned is audio/pcm in a signed 16-bit, 1 channel (mono), little-endian format.

- If you request `json` as the `OutputFormat`, the `ContentType` returned is audio/json.

** RequestCharacters **
Number of characters synthesized.

The response returns the following as the HTTP body.

** AudioStream **
Stream containing the synthesized speech.

Errors

InvalidSampleRateException
The specified sample rate is not valid.
HTTP Status Code: 400

InvalidSsmlException
The SSML you provided is invalid. Verify the SSML syntax, spelling of tags and values, and then try again.
HTTP Status Code: 400

LexiconNotFoundException
Amazon Polly can't find the specified lexicon. This could be caused by a lexicon that is missing, its name is misspelled or specifying a lexicon that is in a different region.
Verify that the lexicon exists, is in the region (see ListLexicons) and that you spelled its name is spelled correctly. Then try again.
HTTP Status Code: 404

MarksNotSupportedForFormatException
Speech marks are not supported for the `OutputFormat` selected. Speech marks are only available for content in `json` format.
HTTP Status Code: 400

ServiceFailureException
An unknown condition has caused a service failure.
HTTP Status Code: 500

SsmlMarksNotSupportedForTextTypeException
SSML speech marks are not supported for plain text-type input.
HTTP Status Code: 400

TextLengthExceededException
The value of the "Text" parameter is longer than the accepted limits. The limit for input text is a maximum of 3000 characters total, of which no more than 1500 can be billed characters. SSML tags are not counted as billed characters.
HTTP Status Code: 400

See Also

For more information about using this API in one of the language-specific AWS SDKs, see the following:

- AWS Command Line Interface
- AWS SDK for .NET
- AWS SDK for C++
- AWS SDK for Go
- AWS SDK for Java
- AWS SDK for JavaScript
- AWS SDK for PHP V3
- AWS SDK for Python
- AWS SDK for Ruby V2

Python Samples

The following code samples show how to use Python (boto3)-based applications to accomplish various tasks with Amazon Polly. These samples are not intended to be full examples, but can be included in larger Python applications that use the AWS SDK for Python (Boto).

- PutLexicon
- GetLexicon
- ListLexicon
- DeleteLexicon

ListLexicon

The following Python code example uses the AWS SDK for Python (Boto) to list the lexicons in your account in the region specified in your local AWS configuration. For information about creating the configuration file, see Step 3.1: Set Up the AWS Command Line Interface (AWS CLI).

```python
import sys

from boto3 import Session
from botocore.exceptions import BotoCoreError, ClientError

# Create a client using the credentials and region defined in the adminuser
# section of the AWS credentials and configuration files
session = Session(profile_name="adminuser")
polly = session.client("polly")

try:
    # Request the list of available lexicons
    response = polly.list_lexicons()
except (BotoCoreError, ClientError) as error:
    # The service returned an error, exit gracefully
    print(error)
    sys.exit(-1)

# Get the list of lexicons in the response
lexicons = response.get("Lexicons", [])
print("{0} lexicon(s) found".format(len(lexicons)))

# Output a formatted list of lexicons with some of the attributes
for lexicon in lexicons:
    print((u" - {Name} ({Attributes[LanguageCode]}), "
           "{Attributes[LexemesCount]} lexeme(s)").format(**lexicon))
```

Example Applications

This section contains additional examples, in the form of example applications which can be used to explore Amazon Polly.

- Python Example (HTML5 Client and Python Server)
- Java Example
- iOS Example
- Android Example

Python Example (HTML5 Client and Python Server)

This example application consists of the following:

- An HTTP 1.1 server using the HTTP chunked transfer coding (see Chunked Transfer Coding)

- A simple HTML5 user interface that interacts with the HTTP 1.1 server (shown below):

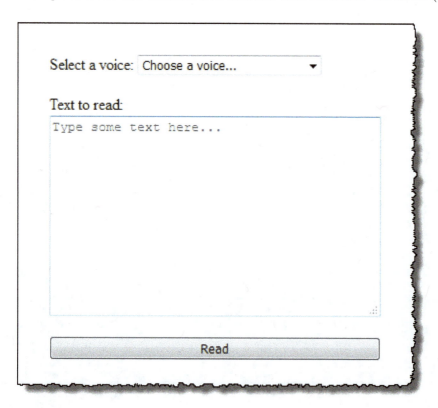

The goal of this example is to show how to use Amazon Polly to stream speech from a browser-based HTML5 application. Consuming the audio stream produced by Amazon Polly as the text gets synthesized is the recommended approach for use cases where responsiveness is an important factor (for example, dialog systems, screen readers, etc.).

To run this example application you need the following:

- Web browser compliant with the HTML5 and EcmaScript5 standards (for example, Chrome 23.0 or higher, Firefox 21.0 or higher, Internet Explorer 9.0, or higher)

- Python version greater than 3.0

To test the application

1. Save the server code as `server.py`. For the code, see Python Example: Python Server Code (server.py).

2. Save the HTML5 client code as `index.html`. For the code, see Python Example: HTML5 User Interface (index.html).

3. Run the following command from the path where you saved server.py to start the application (on some systems you might need to use `python3` instead of `python` when running the command).

```
1 $ python  server.py
```

After the application starts, a URL appears on the terminal.

4. Open the URL shown in the terminal in a web browser.

    You can pass the address and port for the application server to use as a parameter to `server.py`. For more information, run `python server.py -h`.

5. To listen to speech, choose a voice from the list, type some text, and then choose **Read**. The speech starts playing as soon as Amazon Polly transfers the first usable chunk of audio data.

6. To stop the Python server when you're finished testing the application, press Ctrl+C in the terminal where the server is running.

Note

The server creates a Boto3 client using the AWS SDK for Python (Boto). The client uses the credentials stored in the AWS config file on your computer to sign and authenticate the requests to Amazon Polly. For more information on how to create the AWS config file and store credentials, see Configuring the AWS Command Line Interface in the *AWS Command Line Interface User Guide*.

Python Example: HTML5 User Interface (index.html)

This section provides the code for the HTML5 client described in Python Example (HTML5 Client and Python Server).

```
1  <html>
2
3  <head>
4      <title>Text-to-Speech Example Application</title>
5      <script>
6          /*
7           * This sample code requires a web browser with support for both the
8           * HTML5 and ECMAScript 5 standards; the following is a non-comprehensive
9           * list of compliant browsers and their minimum version:
10          *
11          * - Chrome 23.0+
12          * - Firefox 21.0+
13          * - Internet Explorer 9.0+
14          * - Edge 12.0+
15          * - Opera 15.0+
16          * - Safari 6.1+
17          * - Android (stock web browser) 4.4+
18          * - Chrome for Android 51.0+
19          * - Firefox for Android 48.0+
20          * - Opera Mobile 37.0+
21          * - iOS (Safari Mobile and Chrome) 3.2+
22          * - Internet Explorer Mobile 10.0+
23          * - Blackberry Browser 10.0+
24          */
25
26          // Mapping of the OutputFormat parameter of the SynthesizeSpeech API
27          // and the audio format strings understood by the browser
28          var AUDIO_FORMATS = {
29              'ogg_vorbis': 'audio/ogg',
30              'mp3': 'audio/mpeg',
31              'pcm': 'audio/wave; codecs=1'
32          };
33
34          /**
35           * Handles fetching JSON over HTTP
36           */
37          function fetchJSON(method, url, onSuccess, onError) {
38              var request = new XMLHttpRequest();
39              request.open(method, url, true);
40              request.onload = function () {
41                  // If loading is complete
42                  if (request.readyState === 4) {
43                      // if the request was successful
44                      if (request.status === 200) {
45                          var data;
46
47                          // Parse the JSON in the response
48                          try {
49                              data = JSON.parse(request.responseText);
```

```
50          } catch (error) {
51              onError(request.status, error.toString());
52          }
53
54          onSuccess(data);
55        } else {
56          onError(request.status, request.responseText)
57        }
58      }
59    };
60
61    request.send();
62  }
63
64  /**
65   * Returns a list of audio formats supported by the browser
66   */
67  function getSupportedAudioFormats(player) {
68    return Object.keys(AUDIO_FORMATS)
69      .filter(function (format) {
70        var supported = player.canPlayType(AUDIO_FORMATS[format]);
71        return supported === 'probably' || supported === 'maybe';
72      });
73  }
74
75  // Initialize the application when the DOM is loaded and ready to be
76  // manipulated
77  document.addEventListener("DOMContentLoaded", function () {
78    var input = document.getElementById('input'),
79        voiceMenu = document.getElementById('voice'),
80        text = document.getElementById('text'),
81        player = document.getElementById('player'),
82        submit = document.getElementById('submit'),
83        supportedFormats = getSupportedAudioFormats(player);
84
85    // Display a message and don't allow submitting the form if the
86    // browser doesn't support any of the available audio formats
87    if (supportedFormats.length === 0) {
88      submit.disabled = true;
89      alert('The web browser in use does not support any of the' +
90            ' available audio formats. Please try with a different' +
91            ' one.');
92    }
93
94    // Play the audio stream when the form is submitted successfully
95    input.addEventListener('submit', function (event) {
96      // Validate the fields in the form, display a message if
97      // unexpected values are encountered
98      if (voiceMenu.selectedIndex <= 0 || text.value.length === 0) {
99        alert('Please fill in all the fields.');
100       } else {
101         var selectedVoice = voiceMenu
102                                 .options[voiceMenu.selectedIndex]
103                                 .value;
```

```
104
105             // Point the player to the streaming server
106             player.src = '/read?voiceId=' +
107                 encodeURIComponent(selectedVoice) +
108                 '&text=' + encodeURIComponent(text.value) +
109                 '&outputFormat=' + supportedFormats[0];
110             player.play();
111         }
112
113         // Stop the form from submitting,
114         // Submitting the form is allowed only if the browser doesn't
115         // support Javascript to ensure functionality in such a case
116         event.preventDefault();
117     });
118
119     // Load the list of available voices and display them in a menu
120     fetchJSON('GET', '/voices',
121         // If the request succeeds
122         function (voices) {
123             var container = document.createDocumentFragment();
124
125             // Build the list of options for the menu
126             voices.forEach(function (voice) {
127                 var option = document.createElement('option');
128                 option.value = voice['Id'];
129                 option.innerHTML = voice['Name'] + ' (' +
130                     voice['Gender'] + ', ' +
131                     voice['LanguageName'] + ')';
132                 container.appendChild(option);
133             });
134
135             // Add the options to the menu and enable the form field
136             voiceMenu.appendChild(container);
137             voiceMenu.disabled = false;
138         },
139         // If the request fails
140         function (status, response) {
141             // Display a message in case loading data from the server
142             // fails
143             alert(status + ' - ' + response);
144         });
145     });
146
147 </script>
148 <style>
149     #input {
150         min-width: 100px;
151         max-width: 600px;
152         margin: 0 auto;
153         padding: 50px;
154     }
155
156     #input div {
157         margin-bottom: 20px;
```

```
158            }
159
160        #text {
161            width: 100%;
162            height: 200px;
163            display: block;
164        }
165
166        #submit {
167            width: 100%;
168        }
169    </style>
170 </head>
171
172 <body>
173    <form id="input" method="GET" action="/read">
174        <div>
175            <label for="voice">Select a voice:</label>
176            <select id="voice" name="voiceId" disabled>
177                <option value="">Choose a voice...</option>
178            </select>
179        </div>
180        <div>
181            <label for="text">Text to read:</label>
182            <textarea id="text" maxlength="1000" minlength="1" name="text"
183                    placeholder="Type some text here..."></textarea>
184        </div>
185        <input type="submit" value="Read" id="submit" />
186    </form>
187    <audio id="player"></audio>
188 </body>
189
190 </html>
```

Python Example: Python Server Code (server.py)

This section provides the code for the Python server described in Python Example (HTML5 Client and Python Server).

```python
"""
Example Python 2.7+/3.3+ Application

This application consists of a HTTP 1.1 server using the HTTP chunked transfer
coding (https://tools.ietf.org/html/rfc2616#section-3.6.1) and a minimal HTML5
user interface that interacts with it.

The goal of this example is to start streaming the speech to the client (the
HTML5 web UI) as soon as the first consumable chunk of speech is returned in
order to start playing the audio as soon as possible.
For use cases where low latency and responsiveness are strong requirements,
this is the recommended approach.

The service documentation contains examples for non-streaming use cases where
waiting for the speech synthesis to complete and fetching the whole audio stream
at once are an option.

To test the application, run 'python server.py' and then open the URL
displayed in the terminal in a web browser (see index.html for a list of
supported browsers). The address and port for the server can be passed as
parameters to server.py. For more information, run: 'python server.py -h'
"""
from argparse import ArgumentParser
from collections import namedtuple
from contextlib import closing
from io import BytesIO
from json import dumps as json_encode
import os
import sys

if sys.version_info >= (3, 0):
    from http.server import BaseHTTPRequestHandler, HTTPServer
    from socketserver import ThreadingMixIn
    from urllib.parse import parse_qs
else:
    from BaseHTTPServer import BaseHTTPRequestHandler, HTTPServer
    from SocketServer import ThreadingMixIn
    from urlparse import parse_qs

from boto3 import Session
from botocore.exceptions import BotoCoreError, ClientError

ResponseStatus = namedtuple("HTTPStatus",
                            ["code", "message"])

ResponseData = namedtuple("ResponseData",
                          ["status", "content_type", "data_stream"])

# Mapping the output format used in the client to the content type for the
```

```python
50  # response
51  AUDIO_FORMATS = {"ogg_vorbis": "audio/ogg",
52                  "mp3": "audio/mpeg",
53                  "pcm": "audio/wave; codecs=1"}
54  CHUNK_SIZE = 1024
55  HTTP_STATUS = {"OK": ResponseStatus(code=200, message="OK"),
56                 "BAD_REQUEST": ResponseStatus(code=400, message="Bad request"),
57                 "NOT_FOUND": ResponseStatus(code=404, message="Not found"),
58                 "INTERNAL_SERVER_ERROR": ResponseStatus(code=500, message="Internal server error
                      ")}
59  PROTOCOL = "http"
60  ROUTE_INDEX = "/index.html"
61  ROUTE_VOICES = "/voices"
62  ROUTE_READ = "/read"
63
64
65  # Create a client using the credentials and region defined in the adminuser
66  # section of the AWS credentials and configuration files
67  session = Session(profile_name="adminuser")
68  polly = session.client("polly")
69
70
71  class HTTPStatusError(Exception):
72      """Exception wrapping a value from http.server.HTTPStatus"""
73
74      def __init__(self, status, description=None):
75          """
76          Constructs an error instance from a tuple of
77          (code, message, description), see http.server.HTTPStatus
78          """
79          super(HTTPStatusError, self).__init__()
80          self.code = status.code
81          self.message = status.message
82          self.explain = description
83
84
85  class ThreadedHTTPServer(ThreadingMixIn, HTTPServer):
86      """An HTTP Server that handle each request in a new thread"""
87      daemon_threads = True
88
89
90  class ChunkedHTTPRequestHandler(BaseHTTPRequestHandler):
91      """HTTP 1.1 Chunked encoding request handler"""
92      # Use HTTP 1.1 as 1.0 doesn't support chunked encoding
93      protocol_version = "HTTP/1.1"
94
95      def query_get(self, queryData, key, default=""):
96          """Helper for getting values from a pre-parsed query string"""
97          return queryData.get(key, [default])[0]
98
99      def do_GET(self):
100         """Handles GET requests"""
101
102         # Extract values from the query string
```

```python
103            path, _, query_string = self.path.partition('?')
104            query = parse_qs(query_string)
105
106            response = None
107
108            print(u"[START]: Received GET for %s with query: %s" % (path, query))
109
110            try:
111                # Handle the possible request paths
112                if path == ROUTE_INDEX:
113                    response = self.route_index(path, query)
114                elif path == ROUTE_VOICES:
115                    response = self.route_voices(path, query)
116                elif path == ROUTE_READ:
117                    response = self.route_read(path, query)
118                else:
119                    response = self.route_not_found(path, query)
120
121                self.send_headers(response.status, response.content_type)
122                self.stream_data(response.data_stream)
123
124            except HTTPStatusError as err:
125                # Respond with an error and log debug
126                # information
127                if sys.version_info >= (3, 0):
128                    self.send_error(err.code, err.message, err.explain)
129                else:
130                    self.send_error(err.code, err.message)
131
132                self.log_error(u"%s %s %s - [%d] %s", self.client_address[0],
133                               self.command, self.path, err.code, err.explain)
134
135        print("[END]")
136
137    def route_not_found(self, path, query):
138        """Handles routing for unexpected paths"""
139        raise HTTPStatusError(HTTP_STATUS["NOT_FOUND"], "Page not found")
140
141    def route_index(self, path, query):
142        """Handles routing for the application's entry point'"""
143        try:
144            return ResponseData(status=HTTP_STATUS["OK"], content_type="text_html",
145                                # Open a binary stream for reading the index
146                                # HTML file
147                                data_stream=open(os.path.join(sys.path[0],
148                                                              path[1:]), "rb"))
149        except IOError as err:
150            # Couldn't open the stream
151            raise HTTPStatusError(HTTP_STATUS["INTERNAL_SERVER_ERROR"],
152                                  str(err))
153
154    def route_voices(self, path, query):
155        """Handles routing for listing available voices"""
156        params = {}
```

```
157        voices = []
158
159        while True:
160            try:
161                # Request list of available voices, if a continuation token
162                # was returned by the previous call then use it to continue
163                # listing
164                response = polly.describe_voices(**params)
165            except (BotoCoreError, ClientError) as err:
166                # The service returned an error
167                raise HTTPStatusError(HTTP_STATUS["INTERNAL_SERVER_ERROR"],
168                                      str(err))
169
170            # Collect all the voices
171            voices.extend(response.get("Voices", []))
172
173            # If a continuation token was returned continue, stop iterating
174            # otherwise
175            if "NextToken" in response:
176                params = {"NextToken": response["NextToken"]}
177            else:
178                break
179
180        json_data = json_encode(voices)
181        bytes_data = bytes(json_data, "utf-8") if sys.version_info >= (3, 0) \
182            else bytes(json_data)
183
184        return ResponseData(status=HTTP_STATUS["OK"],
185                            content_type="application/json",
186                            # Create a binary stream for the JSON data
187                            data_stream=BytesIO(bytes_data))
188
189    def route_read(self, path, query):
190        """Handles routing for reading text (speech synthesis)"""
191        # Get the parameters from the query string
192        text = self.query_get(query, "text")
193        voiceId = self.query_get(query, "voiceId")
194        outputFormat = self.query_get(query, "outputFormat")
195
196        # Validate the parameters, set error flag in case of unexpected
197        # values
198        if len(text) == 0 or len(voiceId) == 0 or \
199                outputFormat not in AUDIO_FORMATS:
200            raise HTTPStatusError(HTTP_STATUS["BAD_REQUEST"],
201                                  "Wrong parameters")
202        else:
203            try:
204                # Request speech synthesis
205                response = polly.synthesize_speech(Text=text,
206                                                   VoiceId=voiceId,
207                                                   OutputFormat=outputFormat)
208            except (BotoCoreError, ClientError) as err:
209                # The service returned an error
210                raise HTTPStatusError(HTTP_STATUS["INTERNAL_SERVER_ERROR"],
```

```python
211                             str(err))
212
213               return ResponseData(status=HTTP_STATUS["OK"],
214                             content_type=AUDIO_FORMATS[outputFormat],
215                             # Access the audio stream in the response
216                             data_stream=response.get("AudioStream"))
217
218       def send_headers(self, status, content_type):
219           """Send out the group of headers for a successful request"""
220           # Send HTTP headers
221           self.send_response(status.code, status.message)
222           self.send_header('Content-type', content_type)
223           self.send_header('Transfer-Encoding', 'chunked')
224           self.send_header('Connection', 'close')
225           self.end_headers()
226
227       def stream_data(self, stream):
228           """Consumes a stream in chunks to produce the response's output'"""
229           print("Streaming started...")
230
231           if stream:
232               # Note: Closing the stream is important as the service throttles on
233               # the number of parallel connections. Here we are using
234               # contextlib.closing to ensure the close method of the stream object
235               # will be called automatically at the end of the with statement's
236               # scope.
237               with closing(stream) as managed_stream:
238                   # Push out the stream's content in chunks
239                   while True:
240                       data = managed_stream.read(CHUNK_SIZE)
241                       self.wfile.write(b"%X\r\n%s\r\n" % (len(data), data))
242
243                       # If there's no more data to read, stop streaming
244                       if not data:
245                           break
246
247                   # Ensure any buffered output has been transmitted and close the
248                   # stream
249                   self.wfile.flush()
250
251               print("Streaming completed.")
252           else:
253               # The stream passed in is empty
254               self.wfile.write(b"0\r\n\r\n")
255               print("Nothing to stream.")
256
257 # Define and parse the command line arguments
258 cli = ArgumentParser(description='Example Python Application')
259 cli.add_argument(
260     "-p", "--port", type=int, metavar="PORT", dest="port", default=8000)
261 cli.add_argument(
262     "--host", type=str, metavar="HOST", dest="host", default="localhost")
263 arguments = cli.parse_args()
264
```

```
265  # If the module is invoked directly, initialize the application
266  if __name__ == '__main__':
267      # Create and configure the HTTP server instance
268      server = ThreadedHTTPServer((arguments.host, arguments.port),
269                                  ChunkedHTTPRequestHandler)
270      print("Starting server, use <Ctrl-C> to stop...")
271      print(u"Open {0}://{1}:{2}{3} in a web browser.".format(PROTOCOL,
272                                                      arguments.host,
273                                                      arguments.port,
274                                                      ROUTE_INDEX))
275
276      try:
277          # Listen for requests indefinitely
278          server.serve_forever()
279      except KeyboardInterrupt:
280          # A request to terminate has been received, stop the server
281          print("\nShutting down...")
282          server.socket.close()
```

Java Example

This example shows how to use Amazon Polly to stream speech from a Java-based application. The example uses the AWS SDK for Java to read the specified text using a voice selected from a list.

The code shown covers major tasks, but does only minimal error checking. If Amazon Polly encounters an error, the application terminates.

To run this example application, you need the following:

- Java 8 Java Development Kit (JDK)
- AWS SDK for Java
- Apache Maven

To test the application

1. Ensure that the JAVA_HOME environment variable is set for the JDK.

   For example, if you installed JDK 1.8.0_121 on Windows at `C:\Program Files\Java\jdk1.8.0_121`, you would type the following at the command prompt:

   ```
   1 set JAVA_HOME=""C:\Program Files\Java\jdk1.8.0_121""
   ```

   If you installed JDK 1.8.0_121 in Linux at `/usr/lib/jvm/java8-openjdk-amd64` , you would type the following at the command prompt:

   ```
   1 export JAVA_HOME=/usr/lib/jvm/java8-openjdk-amd64
   ```

2. Set the Maven environment variables to run Maven from the command line.

   For example, if you installed Maven 3.3.9 on Windows at `C:\Program Files\apache-maven-3.3.9`, you would type the following:

   ```
   1 set M2_HOME=""C:\Program Files\apache-maven-3.3.9""
   2 set M2=%M2_HOME%\bin
   3 set PATH=%M2%;%PATH%
   ```

   If you installed Maven 3.3.9 on Linux at `/home/ec2-user/opt/apache-maven-3.3.9`, you would type the following:

   ```
   1 export M2_HOME=/home/ec2-user/opt/apache-maven-3.3.9
   2 export M2=$M2_HOME/bin
   3 export PATH=$M2:$PATH
   ```

3. Create a new directory called `polly-java-demo`.

4. In the `polly-java-demo` directory, create a new file called `pom.xml`, and paste the following code into it:

   ```
   1 <project xmlns="http://maven.apache.org/POM/4.0.0"
   2                 xmlns:xsi="http://www.w3.org/2001/XMLSchema-instance"
   3  xsi:schemaLocation="http://maven.apache.org/POM/4.0.0 http://maven.apache.org/xsd/maven
          -4.0.0.xsd">
   4  <modelVersion>4.0.0</modelVersion>
   5  <groupId>com.amazonaws.polly</groupId>
   6  <artifactId>java-demo</artifactId>
   7  <version>0.0.1-SNAPSHOT</version>
   8
   9  <dependencies>
   10     <!-- https://mvnrepository.com/artifact/com.amazonaws/aws-java-sdk-polly -->
   11     <dependency>
   ```

```
12          <groupId>com.amazonaws</groupId>
13          <artifactId>aws-java-sdk-polly</artifactId>
14          <version>1.11.77</version>
15      </dependency>
16      <!-- https://mvnrepository.com/artifact/com.googlecode.soundlibs/jlayer -->
17      <dependency>
18          <groupId>com.googlecode.soundlibs</groupId>
19          <artifactId>jlayer</artifactId>
20          <version>1.0.1-1</version>
21      </dependency>
22
23  </dependencies>
24  <build>
25      <plugins>
26          <plugin>
27              <groupId>org.codehaus.mojo</groupId>
28              <artifactId>exec-maven-plugin</artifactId>
29              <version>1.2.1</version>
30              <executions>
31                  <execution>
32                      <goals>
33                          <goal>java</goal>
34                      </goals>
35                  </execution>
36              </executions>
37              <configuration>
38                  <mainClass>com.amazonaws.demos.polly.PollyDemo</mainClass>
39              </configuration>
40          </plugin>
41      </plugins>
42  </build>
43 </project>
```

5. Create a new directory called `polly` at `src/main/java/com/amazonaws/demos`.

6. In the `polly` directory, create a new Java source file called `PollyDemo.java`, and paste in the following code:

```
1 package com.amazonaws.demos.polly;
2
3 import java.io.IOException;
4 import java.io.InputStream;
5
6 import com.amazonaws.ClientConfiguration;
7 import com.amazonaws.auth.DefaultAWSCredentialsProviderChain;
8 import com.amazonaws.regions.Region;
9 import com.amazonaws.regions.Regions;
10 import com.amazonaws.services.polly.AmazonPollyClient;
11 import com.amazonaws.services.polly.model.DescribeVoicesRequest;
12 import com.amazonaws.services.polly.model.DescribeVoicesResult;
13 import com.amazonaws.services.polly.model.OutputFormat;
14 import com.amazonaws.services.polly.model.SynthesizeSpeechRequest;
15 import com.amazonaws.services.polly.model.SynthesizeSpeechResult;
16 import com.amazonaws.services.polly.model.Voice;
17
18 import javazoom.jl.player.advanced.AdvancedPlayer;
```

```
19 import javazoom.jl.player.advanced.PlaybackEvent;
20 import javazoom.jl.player.advanced.PlaybackListener;
21
22 public class PollyDemo {
23
24  private final AmazonPollyClient polly;
25  private final Voice voice;
26  private static final String SAMPLE = "Congratulations. You have successfully built this working
         demo
27 of Amazon Polly in Java. Have fun building voice enabled apps with Amazon Polly (that's me!),
      and always
28 look at the AWS website for tips and tricks on using Amazon Polly and other great services from
         AWS";
29
30  public PollyDemo(Region region) {
31     // create an Amazon Polly client in a specific region
32     polly = new AmazonPollyClient(new DefaultAWSCredentialsProviderChain(),
33     new ClientConfiguration());
34     polly.setRegion(region);
35     // Create describe voices request.
36     DescribeVoicesRequest describeVoicesRequest = new DescribeVoicesRequest();
37
38     // Synchronously ask Amazon Polly to describe available TTS voices.
39     DescribeVoicesResult describeVoicesResult = polly.describeVoices(describeVoicesRequest);
40     voice = describeVoicesResult.getVoices().get(0);
41  }
42
43  public InputStream synthesize(String text, OutputFormat format) throws IOException {
44     SynthesizeSpeechRequest synthReq =
45     new SynthesizeSpeechRequest().withText(text).withVoiceId(voice.getId())
46           .withOutputFormat(format);
47     SynthesizeSpeechResult synthRes = polly.synthesizeSpeech(synthReq);
48
49     return synthRes.getAudioStream();
50  }
51
52  public static void main(String args[]) throws Exception {
53     //create the test class
54     PollyDemo helloWorld = new PollyDemo(Region.getRegion(Regions.US_EAST_1));
55     //get the audio stream
56     InputStream speechStream = helloWorld.synthesize(SAMPLE, OutputFormat.Mp3);
57
58     //create an MP3 player
59     AdvancedPlayer player = new AdvancedPlayer(speechStream,
60           javazoom.jl.player.FactoryRegistry.systemRegistry().createAudioDevice());
61
62     player.setPlayBackListener(new PlaybackListener() {
63        @Override
64        public void playbackStarted(PlaybackEvent evt) {
65           System.out.println("Playback started");
66           System.out.println(SAMPLE);
67        }
68
69        @Override
```

```
70        public void playbackFinished(PlaybackEvent evt) {
71            System.out.println("Playback finished");
72        }
73    });
74
75
76    // play it!
77    player.play();
78
79 }
80 }
```

1. Return to the `polly-java-demo` directory to clean, compile, and execute the demo:

```
1 mvn clean compile exec:java
```

iOS Example

The following example uses the iOS SDK for Amazon Polly to read the specified text using a voice selected from a list of voices.

The code shown here covers the major tasks but does not handle errors. For the complete code, see AWS SDK for iOS Amazon Polly demo.

Initialize

```
1  // Region of Amazon Polly.
2  let AwsRegion = AWSRegionType.usEast1
3
4  // Cognito pool ID. Pool needs to be unauthenticated pool with
5  // Amazon Polly permissions.
6  let CognitoIdentityPoolId = "YourCognitoIdentityPoolId"
7
8  // Initialize the Amazon Cognito credentials provider.
9  let credentialProvider = AWSCognitoCredentialsProvider(regionType: AwsRegion, identityPoolId:
       CognitoIdentityPoolId)
10
11 // Create an audio player
12 var audioPlayer = AVPlayer()
```

Get List of Available Voices

```
1  // Use the configuration as default
2  AWSServiceManager.default().defaultServiceConfiguration = configuration
3
4  // Get all the voices (no parameters specified in input) from Amazon Polly
5  // This creates an async task.
6  let task = AWSPolly.default().describeVoices(AWSPollyDescribeVoicesInput())
7
8  // When the request is done, asynchronously do the following block
9  // (we ignore all the errors, but in a real-world scenario they need
10 // to be handled)
11 task.continue(successBlock: { (awsTask: AWSTask) -> Any? in
12     // awsTask.result is an instance of AWSPollyDescribeVoicesOutput in
13     // case of the "describeVoices" method
14     let voices = (awsTask.result! as AWSPollyDescribeVoicesOutput).voices
15
16     return nil
17 })
```

Synthesize Speech

```
1  // First, Amazon Polly requires an input, which we need to prepare.
2  // Again, we ignore the errors, however this should be handled in
3  // real applications. Here we are using the URL Builder Request,
4  // since in order to make the synthesis quicker we will pass the
5  // presigned URL to the system audio player.
6  let input = AWSPollySynthesizeSpeechURLBuilderRequest()
7
8  // Text to synthesize
9  input.text = "Sample text"
10
11 // We expect the output in MP3 format
```

```
12 input.outputFormat = AWSPollyOutputFormat.mp3
13
14 // Choose the voice ID
15 input.voiceId = AWSPollyVoiceId.joanna
16
17 // Create an task to synthesize speech using the given synthesis input
18 let builder = AWSPollySynthesizeSpeechURLBuilder.default().getPreSignedURL(input)
19
20 // Request the URL for synthesis result
21 builder.continueOnSuccessWith(block: { (awsTask: AWSTask<NSURL>) -> Any? in
22     // The result of getPresignedURL task is NSURL.
23     // Again, we ignore the errors in the example.
24     let url = awsTask.result!
25
26     // Try playing the data using the system AVAudioPlayer
27     self.audioPlayer.replaceCurrentItem(with: AVPlayerItem(url: url as URL))
28     self.audioPlayer.play()
29
30     return nil
31 })
```

Android Example

The following example uses the Android SDK for Amazon Polly to read the specified text using a voice selected from a list of voices.

The code shown here covers the major tasks but does not handle errors. For the complete code, see the AWS SDK for Android Amazon Polly demo.

Initialize

```
1  // Cognito pool ID. Pool needs to be unauthenticated pool with
2  // Amazon Polly permissions.
3  String COGNITO_POOL_ID = "YourCognitoIdentityPoolId";
4
5  // Region of Amazon Polly.
6  Regions MY_REGION = Regions.US_EAST_1;
7
8  // Initialize the Amazon Cognito credentials provider.
9  CognitoCachingCredentialsProvider credentialsProvider = new CognitoCachingCredentialsProvider(
10         getApplicationContext(),
11         COGNITO_POOL_ID,
12         MY_REGION
13 );
14
15 // Create a client that supports generation of presigned URLs.
16 AmazonPollyPresigningClient client = new AmazonPollyPresigningClient(credentialsProvider);
```

Get List of Available Voices

```
1  // Create describe voices request.
2  DescribeVoicesRequest describeVoicesRequest = new DescribeVoicesRequest();
3
4  // Synchronously ask Amazon Polly to describe available TTS voices.
5  DescribeVoicesResult describeVoicesResult = client.describeVoices(describeVoicesRequest);
6  List<Voice> voices = describeVoicesResult.getVoices();
```

Get URL for Audio Stream

```
1  // Create speech synthesis request.
2  SynthesizeSpeechPresignRequest synthesizeSpeechPresignRequest =
3         new SynthesizeSpeechPresignRequest()
4         // Set the text to synthesize.
5         .withText("Hello world!")
6         // Select voice for synthesis.
7         .withVoiceId(voices.get(0).getId()) // "Joanna"
8         // Set format to MP3.
9         .withOutputFormat(OutputFormat.Mp3);
10
11 // Get the presigned URL for synthesized speech audio stream.
12 URL presignedSynthesizeSpeechUrl =
13         client.getPresignedSynthesizeSpeechUrl(synthesizeSpeechPresignRequest);
```

Play Synthesized Speech

```
1  // Use MediaPlayer: https://developer.android.com/guide/topics/media/mediaplayer.html
2
3  // Create a media player to play the synthesized audio stream.
```

160

```java
4 MediaPlayer mediaPlayer = new MediaPlayer();
5 mediaPlayer.setAudioStreamType(AudioManager.STREAM_MUSIC);
6
7 try {
8     // Set media player's data source to previously obtained URL.
9     mediaPlayer.setDataSource(presignedSynthesizeSpeechUrl.toString());
10 } catch (IOException e) {
11     Log.e(TAG, "Unable to set data source for the media player! " + e.getMessage());
12 }
13
14 // Prepare the MediaPlayer asynchronously (since the data source is a network stream).
15 mediaPlayer.prepareAsync();
16
17 // Set the callback to start the MediaPlayer when it's prepared.
18 mediaPlayer.setOnPreparedListener(new MediaPlayer.OnPreparedListener() {
19     @Override
20     public void onPrepared(MediaPlayer mp) {
21         mp.start();
22     }
23 });
24
25 // Set the callback to release the MediaPlayer after playback is completed.
26 mediaPlayer.setOnCompletionListener(new MediaPlayer.OnCompletionListener() {
27     @Override
28     public void onCompletion(MediaPlayer mp) {
29     mp.release();
30     }
31 });
```

WordPress Plugin for Amazon Polly

The Amazon Polly plugin for WordPress lets visitors to your WordPress website listen to content in your chosen language and voice. You use the plugin to create an audio file of your written content, which your users can stream at their convenience. Website visitors can consume your content using new channels, such as inline audio players and mobile applications. .

You use the native WordPress **Add Plugins** page to install and configure the plugin. After you install and activate the plugin, you navigate to the Amazon Polly **Settings** page and connect the plugin to your AWS account. You can configure the plugin to automatically create audio files for new content upon publication, or choose the content individually. Archived content can be batch processed to provide your consumers with an enhanced experience as well. You can also use the Amazon Pollycast RSS feed to podcast the new audio content.

Note
In the following procedures, instructions for tasks performed in WordPress might not match the WordPress user interface exactly.

- Installing the Plugin
- Storing Audio Files

Installing the Plugin

Setting up the Amazon Polly plugin for WordPress requires that you have an active AWS account in addition to your working WordPress installation. If you don't have an account, see Step 1.1: Sign up for AWS. When you have an AWS account, follow these steps to finish setting up the plugin:

1. Create a Permissions Policy

2. Create an IAM User for the Plugin

3. Installing and Configuring the Plugin

Create a Permissions Policy

In the AWS Management Console, create an IAM permissions policy called *PollyForWordPressPolicy* using the following code:

```
{
    "Version": "2012-10-17",
    "Statement": [use
        {
            "Sid": ""Permissions1,
            "Effect": "Allow",
            "Action": [
                "polly:SynthesizeSpeech",
                "s3:HeadBucket",
                "polly:DescribeVoices"
            ],
            "Resource": "*"
        },
        {
            "Sid": ""Permissions2,
            "Effect": "Allow",
            "Action": [
                "s3:ListBucket",
                "s3:GetBucketAcl",
                "s3:GetBucketPolicy",
                "s3:"PutObject,
                            "s3:"DeleteObject,
                "s3:CreateBucket",
                "s3:PutObjectAcl"
            ],
            "Resource": "arn:aws:s3:::audio_for_wordpress*"
        }
    ]
}
```

For more information on creating a permissions policy, see Creating Customer-Managed Policies.

Create an IAM User for the Plugin

To connect the plugin to your AWS account, you need to create an AWS Identity and Access Management (IAM) user, then attach the permissions policy to that user. If you deployed WordPress on Amazon EC2, you can skip this step and use the IAM role instead of an individual IAM user. For more information, see: IAM Roles for Amazon EC2 in the *Amazon EC2 User Guide.*

To create an IAM user

1. Open the IAM console at https://console.aws.amazon.com/iam/ and choose **Users**.

2. Choose **Add User**.

3. For **User Name**, type **WordPress**.

4. For **Access Type**, choose **Programmatic access**, then choose **Next: Permissions**.

5. Choose **Attach existing policies direction**. Choose your newly created policy (*PollyForWordPressPolicy*) from the list, then choose **Next: Review**.

6. Choose **Create User**.

7. Copy the **Access key ID** and **Secret access key**. You need them to configure the plugin. **Important** This is the only time you can access these keys, so be sure to record them.

Installing and Configuring the Plugin

To install and configure the plugin

1. Download the Amazon Polly plugin for WordPress from the Amazon Polly plugin GitHub site.

2. On the **WordPress Admin** page, choose **Add New Plugin**, then install and activate the plugin.

3. On the **WordPress Admin** page, choose **Settings**, then for **Amazon Polly Settings**, configure the plugin:

   - **AWS access key and AWS secret key**—AWS credentials, which allow the plugin to use Amazon Polly and Amazon Simple Storage Service (Amazon S3). If you are hosting your WordPress site on Amazon Elastic Compute Cloud (Amazon EC2), you can use AWS Identity and Access Management (IAM) roles instead of credentials. In that case, leave these two fields blank.

   - **Sample rate**—The sample rate of the audio files that will be generated, in Hz. Higher sampling rates mean higher quality audio.

   - **Voice name**—The Amazon Polly voice to use to create the audio file.

   - **Player position**—Where to position the audio player on the website. You can put it before or after the post, or not use it at all. If you want to make your files available as podcasts, using Amazon Pollycast, choose to not display the audio player.

   - **New post default**—Specifies whether Amazon Polly is automatically enabled for all new posts. Choose this option if you want Amazon Polly to use the configuration settings to create an audio file for each new post.

   - **Autoplay**—Specifies whether the audio player automatically starts playing the audio when a user visits an individual post on the website.

   - **Store audio in Amazon S3**—If you want to store audio files in an S3 bucket instead of on the server, choose this option. Amazon Polly creates the bucket for you. For more information and pricing, see Amazon S3.

   - **Amazon CloudFront (CDN) domain name**—If you want to broadcast your audio files with Amazon CloudFront, provide the name of your CloudFront domain, which the plugin will use for streaming audio. You must first create the domain in Amazon CloudFront.

   - **ITunes category**—The category for your podcast. Choosing a category makes it easier for podcast users to find your podcast in the podcast catalog.

- **ITunes explicit**—Specifies whether to enable Amazon Pollycast podcasting.

- **Bulk update all posts**—If you want to convert all posts to use the new plugin settings, choose this option.

4. Choose **Save Changes**

Storing Audio Files

When you publish content on your site, it's sent to Amazon Polly for synthesis. By default, new audio files are stored on your web server. You can also store the files using Amazon S3 or Amazon CloudFront.

The way your WordPress users listen to the audio content on your website depends on where the content is stored:

1. For audio files stored on the WordPress server, files are broadcast directly from the server.

2. For files stored in an Amazon S3 bucket, files are broadcast from the S3 bucket.

3. If you use Amazon CloudFront (CDN), the files are stored on Amazon S3 and are broadcast with Amazon CloudFront.

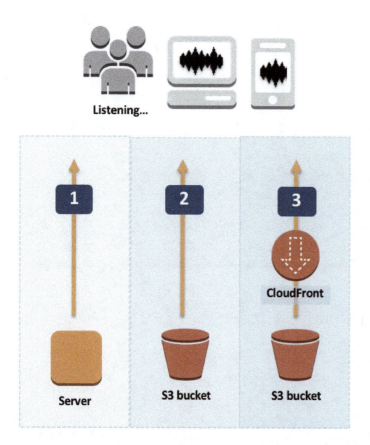

Your users have the same listening experience regardless of how you store your audio files.

Positioning the HTML Player

When you install the Amazon Polly plugin, it displays an HTML player on your WordPress website.

You can use the **Player position** option when configuring the plugin on the **Amazon Polly Settings** page to display the player above or below your text, or not display it at all. For more information about setting configuration options, see Installing and Configuring the Plugin.

Podcasting with Amazon Pollycast

To let users listen to your audio content using standard podcast applications, set up Pollycast feeds. RSS 2.0-compliant Pollycast feeds provide the necessary XML data for aggregation by popular podcast mobile applications and podcast directories, such as iTunes. The Amazon Polly plugin automatically adds Amazon Pollycast endpoints to all WordPress archive URLs. This lets you syndicate both site-wide or targeted podcasts.

You can also add Amazon Pollycast endpoints manually by adding `/amazon-pollycast/` to the URL for a page in a podcasting application. For example:

```
1 example.com/amazon-pollycast/
2 example.com/category/news/amazon-pollycast/
3 example.com/author/john/amazon-pollcast/
```

Amazon Polly Reference

This section provides additional reference material for the Amazon Polly documentation.

- Available Voices
- Languages Supported by Amazon Polly

Available Voices

The following voices are available when using Amazon Polly

Name/ID	Gender
Danish (da-DK)	
Mads	Male
Naja	Female
Dutch (nl-NL)	
Lotte	Female
Ruben	Male
English (Australian) (en-AU)	
Nicole	Female
Russell	Male
English (British) (en-GB)	
Amy	Female
Brian	Male
Emma	Female
English (Indian) (en-IN)	
Aditi	Female
Raveena	Female
English (US) (en-US)	
Ivy	Female
Joanna	Female
Joey	Male
Justin	Male
Kendra	Female
Kimberly	Female
Matthew	Male
Salli	Female
English (Welsh) (en-GB-WLS)	
Geraint	Male
French (fr-FR)	
Céline/Celine	Female
Mathieu	Male
French (Canadian) (fr-CA)	
Chantal	Female
German (de-DE)	
Hans	Male
Marlene	Female
Vicki	Female
Icelandic (is-IS)	
Dóra/Dora	Female
Karl	Male
Italian (it-IT)	
Carla	Female
Giorgio	Male
Japanese (ja-JP)	
Mizuki	Female
Takumi	Male
Korean (ko-KR)	
Seoyeon	Female
Norwegian (nb-NO)	
Liv	Female

Name/ID	Gender
Polish (pl-PL)	
Jacek	Male
Jan	Male
Ewa	Female
Maja	Female
Portuguese (Brazilian) (pt-BR)	
Ricardo	Male
Vitória/Vitoria	Female
Portuguese (European) (pt-PT)	
Cristiano	Male
Inês/Ines	Female
Romanian (ro-RO)	
Carmen	Female
Russian (ru-RU)	
Maxim	Male
Tatyana	Female
Spanish (Castilian) (es-ES)	
Conchita	Female
Enrique	Male
Spanish (Latin American) (es-US)	
Miguel	Male
Penélope/Penelope	Female
Swedish (sv-SE)	
Astrid	Female
Turkish (tr-TR)	
Filiz	Female
Welsh (cy-GB)	
Gwyneth	Female

Languages Supported by Amazon Polly

Language	Language Code
Danish	da-DK
Dutch	nl-NL
English (Australian)	en-AU
English (British)	en-GB
English (Indian)	en-IN
English (US)	en-US
English (Welsh)	en-GB-WLS
French	fr-FR
French (Canadian)	fr-CA
German	de-DE
Icelandic	is-IS
Italian	it-IT
Japanese	ja-JP
Korean	ko-KR
Norwegian	nb-NO
Polish	pl-PL
Portuguese (Brazilian)	pt-BR
Portuguese (European)	pt-PT
Romanian	ro-RO
Russian	ru-RU
Spanish	es-ES
Spanish (Latin American)	es-US
Swedish	sv-SE
Turkish	tr-TR
Welsh	cy-GB

Limits in Amazon Polly

The following are limits to be aware of when using Amazon Polly.

Supported Regions

For a list of AWS Regions where Amazon Polly is available, see AWS Regions and Endpoints in the *Amazon Web Services General Reference*.

Throttling

- Throttle rate per account: 100 transactions (requests) per second (tps) with a burst limit of 120 tps.

  Concurrent connections per account: 90

- Throttle rate per operation:
  [See the AWS documentation website for more details]

Pronunciation Lexicons

- You can store up to 100 lexicons per account.

- Lexicon names can be an alphanumeric string up to 20 characters long.

- Each lexicon can be up to 4,000 characters in size. (Note that the size of the lexicon affects the latency of the SynthesizeSpeech operation.)

- You can specify up to 100 characters for each or replacement in a lexicon.

For information about using lexicons, see Managing Lexicons.

SynthesizeSpeech API Operation

Note the following limits related to using the SynthesizeSpeech API operation:

- The size of the input text can be up to 1500 billed characters (3000 total characters). SSML tags are not counted as billed characters.

- You can specify up to five lexicons to apply to the input text.

- The output audio stream (synthesis) is limited to 5 minutes, after which, any remaining speech is cut off.

For more information, see SynthesizeSpeech.

Note
Some limitations of the `SynthesizeSpeech` API operation can be bypassed using AWS Batch or other services. For more information on AWS Batch, see What Is AWS Batch?

Speech Synthesis Markup Language (SSML)

Note the following limits related to using SSML:

- The `<audio>`, `<lexicon>`, `<lookup>`, and `<voice>` tags are not supported.

- `<break>` elements can specify a maximum duration of 10 seconds each.

- The `<prosody>` tag doesn't support values for the rate attribute lower than -80%.

For more information, see Using SSML.

Logging Amazon Polly API Calls with AWS CloudTrail

Amazon Polly is integrated with CloudTrail, a service that captures all of the Amazon Polly API calls and delivers the log files to an Amazon S3 bucket that you specify. CloudTrail captures API calls from the Amazon Polly console or from your code to the Amazon Polly APIs. Using the information collected by CloudTrail, you can determine the request that was made to Amazon Polly, the source IP address from which the request was made, who made the request, when it was made, and so on.

To learn more about CloudTrail, including how to configure and enable it, see the AWS CloudTrail User Guide.

Amazon Polly Information in CloudTrail

When CloudTrail logging is enabled in your AWS account, API calls made to Amazon Polly actions are tracked in CloudTrail log files, where they are written with other AWS service records. CloudTrail determines when to create and write to a new file based on a time period and file size.

All Amazon Polly actions are logged by CloudTrail and are documented in the Amazon Polly API Reference. The following actions are supported.

- DeleteLexicon
- DescribeVoices
- GetLexicon
- ListLexicons
- PutLexicon
- SynthesizeSpeech

Every log entry contains information about who generated the request. The user identity information in the log entry helps you determine the following:

- Whether the request was made with root or IAM user credentials
- Whether the request was made with temporary security credentials for a role or federated user
- Whether the request was made by another AWS service

For more information, see the CloudTrail userIdentity Element.

You can store your log files in your Amazon S3 bucket for as long as you want, but you can also define Amazon S3 lifecycle rules to archive or delete log files automatically. By default, your log files are encrypted with Amazon S3 server-side encryption (SSE).

If you want to be notified upon log file delivery, you can configure CloudTrail to publish Amazon SNS notifications when new log files are delivered. For more information, see Configuring Amazon SNS Notifications for CloudTrail.

You can also aggregate Amazon Polly log files from multiple AWS regions and multiple AWS accounts into a single Amazon S3 bucket.

For more information, see Receiving CloudTrail Log Files from Multiple Regions and Receiving CloudTrail Log Files from Multiple Accounts.

Understanding Amazon Polly Log File Entries

CloudTrail log files can contain one or more log entries. Each entry lists multiple JSON-formatted events. A log entry represents a single request from any source and includes information about the requested action, the date and time of the action, request parameters, and so on. Log entries are not an ordered stack trace of the public API calls, so they do not appear in any specific order.

Because of potential confidentiality issues, log entries do not contain the synthesized text. Instead, this text is redacted in the log entry.

The following example shows a CloudTrail log entry that demonstrates the **SynthesizeSpeech**.

```
1  {
2      "Records": [
3          {
4              "awsRegion": "us-east-2",
5              "eventID": "19bd70f7-5e60-4cdc-9825-936c552278ae",
6              "eventName": "SynthesizeSpeech",
7              "eventSource": "tts.amazonaws.com",
8              "eventTime": "2016-11-02T03:49:39Z",
9              "eventType": "AwsApiCall",
10             "eventVersion": "1.05",
11             "recipientAccountId": "123456789012",
12             "requestID": "414288c2-a1af-11e6-b17f-d7cfc06cb461",
13             "requestParameters": {
14                 "lexiconNames": [
15                     "SampleLexicon"
16                 ],
17                 "outputFormat": "mp3",
18                 "sampleRate": "22050",
19                 "text": "*********",
20                 "textType": "text",
21                 "voiceId": "Kendra"
22             },
23             "responseElements": {
24                 "contentType": "audio/mpeg",
25                 "requestCharacters": 25
26             },
27             "sourceIPAddress": "1.2.3.4",
28             "userAgent": "Amazon CLI/Polly 1.10 API 2016-06-10",
29             "userIdentity": {
30                 "accessKeyId": "EXAMPLE_KEY_ID",
31                 "accountId": "123456789012",
32                 "arn": "arn:aws:iam::123456789012:user/Alice",
33                 "principalId": "EX_PRINCIPAL_ID",
34                 "type": "IAMUser",
35                 "userName": "Alice"
36             }
37         }
38
39     ]
40  }
```

The `eventName` element identifies the action that occurred and may include date and version information, such as "SynthesizeSpeech20161128", nevertheless it is still referring to the same public API.

Integrating CloudWatch with Amazon Polly

When you interact with Amazon Polly, it sends the following metrics and dimensions to CloudWatch every minute. You can use the following procedures to view the metrics for Amazon Polly.

You can monitor Amazon Polly using CloudWatch, which collects and processes raw data from Amazon Polly into readable, near real-time metrics. These statistics are recorded for a period of two weeks, so that you can access `historical information` and gain a better perspective on how your web application or service is performing. By default, Amazon Polly metric data is sent to CloudWatch in 1 minute intervals. For more information, see What Is Amazon CloudWatch in the Amazon *CloudWatch User Guide*.

Getting CloudWatch Metrics (Console)

1. Open the CloudWatch console at https://console.aws.amazon.com/cloudwatch/.

2. In the navigation pane, choose **Metrics**.

3. In the ** CloudWatch Metrics by Category** pane, under the metrics category for Amazon Polly, select a metrics category, and then in the upper pane, scroll down to view the full list of metrics.

Getting CloudWatch Metrics (CLI)

The following code display available metrics for Amazon Polly.

```
aws cloudwatch list-metrics --namespace "AWS/Polly"
```

The preceding command returns a list of Amazon Polly metrics similar to the following. The `MetricName` element identifies what the metric is.

```
{
    "Metrics": [
        {
            "Namespace": "AWS/Polly",
            "Dimensions": [
                {
                    "Name": "Operation",
                    "Value": "SynthesizeSpeech"
                }
            ],
            "MetricName": "ResponseLatency"
        },
        {
            "Namespace": "AWS/Polly",
            "Dimensions": [
                {
                    "Name": "Operation",
                    "Value": "SynthesizeSpeech"
                }
            ],
            "MetricName": "RequestCharacters"
        }
```

For more information, see GetMetricStatistics in the *Amazon CloudWatch API Reference*.

Amazon Polly Metrics

Amazon Polly produces the following metrics for each request. These metrics are aggregated and in one minute intervals sent to CloudWatch where they are available.

Metric	Description
RequestCharacters	The number of characters in the request. This is billable characters only and does not include SSML tags. Valid Dimension: Operation Valid Statistics: Minimum, Maximum, Average, SampleCount, Sum Unit: Count
ResponseLatency	The latency between when the request was made and the start of the streaming response. Valid Dimensions: Operation Valid Statistics: Minimum, Maximum, Average, SampleCount Unit: milliseconds
2XXCount	HTTP 200 level code returned upon a successful response. Valid Dimensions: Operation Valid Statistics: Average, SampleCount, Sum Unit: Count
4XXCount	HTTP 400 level error code returned upon an error. For each successful response, a zero (0) is emitted. Valid Dimensions: Operation Valid Statistics: Average, SampleCount, Sum Unit: Count
5XXCount	HTTP 500 level error code returned upon an error. For each successful response, a zero (0) is emitted. Valid Dimensions: Operation Valid Statistics: Average, SampleCount, Sum Unit: Count

Dimensions for Amazon Polly Metrics

Amazon Polly metrics use the AWS/Polly namespace and provide metrics for the following dimension:

Dimension	Description
Operation	Metrics are grouped by the API method they refer to. Possible values are SynthesizeSpeech, PutLexicon, DescribeVoices, etc.

Amazon Polly API Reference

This section contains the Amazon Polly API reference.

Note
Authenticated API calls must be signed using the Signature Version 4 Signing Process. For more information, see Signing AWS API Requests in the *Amazon Web Services General Reference*.

Topics

- Actions
- Data Types

Actions

The following actions are supported:

- DeleteLexicon
- DescribeVoices
- GetLexicon
- ListLexicons
- PutLexicon
- SynthesizeSpeech

Data Types

The following data types are supported:

- Lexicon
- LexiconAttributes
- LexiconDescription
- Voice

Lexicon

Provides lexicon name and lexicon content in string format. For more information, see Pronunciation Lexicon Specification (PLS) Version 1.0.

Contents

Content
Lexicon content in string format. The content of a lexicon must be in PLS format.
Type: String
Required: No

Name
Name of the lexicon.
Type: String
Pattern: [0-9A-Za-z]{1,20}
Required: No

See Also

For more information about using this API in one of the language-specific AWS SDKs, see the following:

- AWS SDK for C++
- AWS SDK for Go
- AWS SDK for Java
- AWS SDK for Ruby V2

LexiconAttributes

Contains metadata describing the lexicon such as the number of lexemes, language code, and so on. For more information, see Managing Lexicons.

Contents

Alphabet
Phonetic alphabet used in the lexicon. Valid values are `ipa` and `x-sampa`.
Type: String
Required: No

LanguageCode
Language code that the lexicon applies to. A lexicon with a language code such as "en" would be applied to all English languages (en-GB, en-US, en-AUS, en-WLS, and so on.
Type: String
Valid Values:`cy-GB | da-DK | de-DE | en-AU | en-GB | en-GB-WLS | en-IN | en-US | es-ES | es-US | fr-CA | fr-FR | is-IS | it-IT | ko-KR | ja-JP | nb-NO | nl-NL | pl-PL | pt-BR | pt-PT | ro-RO | ru-RU | sv-SE | tr-TR`
Required: No

LastModified
Date lexicon was last modified (a timestamp value).
Type: Timestamp
Required: No

LexemesCount
Number of lexemes in the lexicon.
Type: Integer
Required: No

LexiconArn
Amazon Resource Name (ARN) of the lexicon.
Type: String
Required: No

Size
Total size of the lexicon, in characters.
Type: Integer
Required: No

See Also

For more information about using this API in one of the language-specific AWS SDKs, see the following:

- AWS SDK for C++
- AWS SDK for Go
- AWS SDK for Java
- AWS SDK for Ruby V2

LexiconDescription

Describes the content of the lexicon.

Contents

Attributes
Provides lexicon metadata.
Type: LexiconAttributes object
Required: No

Name
Name of the lexicon.
Type: String
Pattern: `[0-9A-Za-z]{1,20}`
Required: No

See Also

For more information about using this API in one of the language-specific AWS SDKs, see the following:

- AWS SDK for C++
- AWS SDK for Go
- AWS SDK for Java
- AWS SDK for Ruby V2

Voice

Description of the voice.

Contents

Gender
Gender of the voice.
Type: String
Valid Values:`Female | Male`
Required: No

Id
Amazon Polly assigned voice ID. This is the ID that you specify when calling the `SynthesizeSpeech` operation.
Type: String
Valid Values:`Geraint | Gwyneth | Mads | Naja | Hans | Marlene | Nicole | Russell | Amy | Brian | Emma | Raveena | Ivy | Joanna | Joey | Justin | Kendra | Kimberly | Matthew | Salli | Conchita | Enrique | Miguel | Penelope | Chantal | Celine | Mathieu | Dora | Karl | Carla | Giorgio | Mizuki | Liv | Lotte | Ruben | Ewa | Jacek | Jan | Maja | Ricardo | Vitoria | Cristiano | Ines | Carmen | Maxim | Tatyana | Astrid | Filiz | Vicki | Takumi | Seoyeon | Aditi`
Required: No

LanguageCode
Language code of the voice.
Type: String
Valid Values:`cy-GB | da-DK | de-DE | en-AU | en-GB | en-GB-WLS | en-IN | en-US | es-ES | es-US | fr-CA | fr-FR | is-IS | it-IT | ko-KR | ja-JP | nb-NO | nl-NL | pl-PL | pt-BR | pt-PT | ro-RO | ru-RU | sv-SE | tr-TR`
Required: No

LanguageName
Human readable name of the language in English.
Type: String
Required: No

Name
Name of the voice (for example, Salli, Kendra, etc.). This provides a human readable voice name that you might display in your application.
Type: String
Required: No

See Also

For more information about using this API in one of the language-specific AWS SDKs, see the following:

- AWS SDK for C++
- AWS SDK for Go
- AWS SDK for Java
- AWS SDK for Ruby V2

Authentication and Access Control for Amazon Polly

Access to Amazon Polly requires credentials. Those credentials must have permissions to access AWS resources, such as an Amazon Polly lexicon or an Amazon Elastic Compute Cloud (Amazon EC2) instance. The following sections provide details on how you can use AWS Identity and Access Management (IAM) and Amazon Polly to help secure access to your resources.

- Authentication
- Access Control

Authentication

You can access AWS as any of the following types of identities:

- **AWS account root user** – When you first create an AWS account, you begin with a single sign-in identity that has complete access to all AWS services and resources in the account. This identity is called the AWS account *root user* and is accessed by signing in with the email address and password that you used to create the account. We strongly recommend that you do not use the root user for your everyday tasks, even the administrative ones. Instead, adhere to the best practice of using the root user only to create your first IAM user. Then securely lock away the root user credentials and use them to perform only a few account and service management tasks.

- **IAM user** – An IAM user is an identity within your AWS account that has specific custom permissions (for example, permissions to create a lexicon in Amazon Polly). You can use an IAM user name and password to sign in to secure AWS webpages like the AWS Management Console, AWS Discussion Forums, or the AWS Support Center.

  In addition to a user name and password, you can also generate access keys for each user. You can use these keys when you access AWS services programmatically, either through one of the several SDKs or by using the AWS Command Line Interface (CLI). The SDK and CLI tools use the access keys to cryptographically sign your request. If you don't use AWS tools, you must sign the request yourself. Amazon Polly supports *Signature Version 4*, a protocol for authenticating inbound API requests. For more information about authenticating requests, see Signature Version 4 Signing Process in the *AWS General Reference*.

- **IAM role** – An IAM role is an IAM identity that you can create in your account that has specific permissions. It is similar to an *IAM user*, but it is not associated with a specific person. An IAM role enables you to obtain temporary access keys that can be used to access AWS services and resources. IAM roles with temporary credentials are useful in the following situations:

  - **Federated user access** – Instead of creating an IAM user, you can use existing user identities from AWS Directory Service, your enterprise user directory, or a web identity provider. These are known as *federated users*. AWS assigns a role to a federated user when access is requested through an identity provider. For more information about federated users, see Federated Users and Roles in the *IAM User Guide*.

  - **AWS service access** – You can use an IAM role in your account to grant an AWS service permissions to access your account's resources. For example, you can create a role that allows Amazon Redshift to access an Amazon S3 bucket on your behalf and then load data from that bucket into an Amazon Redshift cluster. For more information, see Creating a Role to Delegate Permissions to an AWS Service in the *IAM User Guide*.

- **Applications running on Amazon EC2** – You can use an IAM role to manage temporary credentials for applications that are running on an EC2 instance and making AWS API requests. This is preferable to storing access keys within the EC2 instance. To assign an AWS role to an EC2 instance and make it available to all of its applications, you create an instance profile that is attached to the instance. An instance profile contains the role and enables programs that are running on the EC2 instance to get temporary credentials. For more information, see Using an IAM Role to Grant Permissions to Applications Running on Amazon EC2 Instances in the *IAM User Guide*.

Access Control

You can have valid credentials to authenticate your requests, but unless you have permissions you cannot create or access Amazon Polly resources. For example, you must have permissions to create an Amazon Polly lexicon.

The following sections describe how to manage permissions for Amazon Polly. We recommend that you read the overview first.

- Overview of Managing Access Permissions to Your Amazon Polly Resources
- Using Identity-Based Policies (IAM Policies) for Amazon Polly
- Amazon Polly API Permissions: Actions, Permissions, and Resources Reference

Overview of Managing Access Permissions to Your Amazon Polly Resources

Every AWS resource is owned by an AWS account, and permissions to create or access a resource are governed by permissions policies. An account administrator can attach permissions policies to IAM identities (that is, users, groups, and roles), and some services (such as AWS Lambda) also support attaching permissions policies to resources.

Note
An *account administrator* (or administrator user) is a user with administrator privileges. For more information, see IAM Best Practices in the *IAM User Guide*.

When granting permissions, you decide who is getting the permissions, the resources they get permissions for, and the specific actions that you want to allow on those resources.

- Amazon Polly Resources and Operations
- Understanding Resource Ownership
- Managing Access to Resources
- Specifying Policy Elements: Actions, Effects, and Principals
- Specifying Conditions in a Policy

Amazon Polly Resources and Operations

In Amazon Polly, the primary resource is *a lexicon*. In a policy, you use an Amazon Resource Name (ARN) to identify the resource that the policy applies to.

These resources and subresources have unique Amazon Resource Names (ARNs) associated with them, as shown in the following table.

Resource Type	ARN Format
Lexicon	arn:aws:polly:region:account-id:lexicon/LexiconName

Amazon Polly provides a set of operations to work with Amazon Polly resources. For a list of available operations, see Amazon Polly Amazon Polly API Reference.

Understanding Resource Ownership

The AWS account owns the resources that are created in the account, regardless of who created the resources. Specifically, the resource owner is the AWS account of the principal entity (that is, the root account, an IAM user, or an IAM role) that authenticates the resource creation request. The following examples illustrate how this works:

- If you use the root account credentials of your AWS account to create a lexicon, your AWS account is the owner of the resource (in Amazon Polly, the resource is a lexicon).

- If you create an IAM user in your AWS account and grant permissions to create a lexicon to that user, the user can create a lexicon. However, your AWS account, to which the user belongs, owns the lexicon resource.

- If you create an IAM role in your AWS account with permissions to create a lexicon, anyone who can assume the role can create a lexicon. Your AWS account, to which the user belongs, owns the lexicon resource.

Managing Access to Resources

A *permissions policy* describes who has access to what. The following section explains the available options for creating permissions policies.

Note
This section discusses using IAM in the context of Amazon Polly. It doesn't provide detailed information about the IAM service. For complete IAM documentation, see What Is IAM? in the *IAM User Guide*. For information about IAM policy syntax and descriptions, see AWS IAM Policy Reference in the *IAM User Guide*.

Policies attached to an IAM identity are referred to as *identity-based* policies (IAM polices) and policies attached to a resource are referred to as *resource-based* policies. Amazon Polly supports identity-based policies.

- Identity-Based Policies (IAM Policies)
- Resource-Based Policies

Identity-Based Policies (IAM Policies)

You can attach policies to IAM identities. For example, you can do the following:

- **Attach a permissions policy to a user or a group in your account** – To grant a user permissions to create a Amazon Polly resource, such as a lexicon, you can attach a permissions policy to a user or group that the user belongs to.

- **Attach a permissions policy to a role (grant cross-account permissions)** – You can attach an identity-based permissions policy to an IAM role to grant cross-account permissions. For example, the administrator in account A can create a role to grant cross-account permissions to another AWS account (for example, account B) or an AWS service as follows:

  1. Account A administrator creates an IAM role and attaches a permissions policy to the role that grants permissions on resources in account A.

  2. Account A administrator attaches a trust policy to the role identifying account B as the principal who can assume the role.

  3. Account B administrator can then delegate permissions to assume the role to any users in account B. Doing this allows users in account B to create or access resources in account A. The principal in the trust policy can also be an AWS service principal if you want to grant an AWS service permissions to assume the role.

  For more information about using IAM to delegate permissions, see Access Management in the *IAM User Guide*.

The following is an example policy that grants permissions to put and get lexicons as well as to list those lexicons currently available.

Amazon Polly supports Identity-based policies for actions at the resource-level. Therefore, the `Resource` value is indicated by the ARN. For example: `arn:aws:polly:us-east-2:account-id:lexicon/*` as the `Resource` value specifies permissions on all owned lexicons within the `us-east-2` region.

```
1  {
2    "Version": "2012-10-17",
3    "Statement": [{
4      "Sid": "AllowPut-Get-ListActions",
5      "Effect": "Allow",
6      "Action": [
7        "polly:PutLexicon",
8        "polly:GetLexicon",
9        "polly:ListLexicons"],
10     "Resource": "arn:aws:polly:us-east-2:account-id:lexicon/*"
```

```
11        }
12    ]
13 }
```

For more information about using identity-based policies with Amazon Polly, see Using Identity-Based Policies (IAM Policies) for Amazon Polly. For more information about users, groups, roles, and permissions, see Identities (Users, Groups, and Roles) in the *IAM User Guide*.

Resource-Based Policies

Other services, such as Amazon S3, also support resource-based permissions policies. For example, you can attach a policy to an S3 bucket to manage access permissions to that bucket. Amazon Polly doesn't support resource-based policies.

Specifying Policy Elements: Actions, Effects, and Principals

For each Amazon Polly resource, the service defines a set of API operations. To grant permissions for these API operations, Amazon Polly defines a set of actions that you can specify in a policy. Some API operations can require permissions for more than one action in order to perform the API operation. For more information about resources and API operations, see Amazon Polly Resources and Operations and Amazon Polly API Reference.

The following are the most basic policy elements:

- **Resource** – You use an Amazon Resource Name (ARN) to identify the resource that the Identity-based policy applies to. For more information, see Amazon Polly Resources and Operations.

- **Action** – You use action keywords to identify resource operations that you want to allow or deny. For example, you can use `polly:PutLexicon` to add a lexicon to the region.

- **Effect** – You specify the effect, either allow or deny, when the user requests the specific action. If you don't explicitly grant access to (allow) a resource, access is implicitly denied. You can also explicitly deny access to a resource, which you might do to make sure that a user cannot access it, even if a different policy grants access.

- **Principal** – In identity-based policies (IAM policies), the user that the policy is attached to is the implicit principal. For resource-based policies, you specify the user, account, service, or other entity that you want to receive permissions (applies to resource-based policies only). Amazon Polly doesn't support resource-based policies.

To learn more about IAM policy syntax and descriptions, see AWS IAM Policy Reference in the *IAM User Guide*.

For a table showing all of the Amazon Polly API operations and the resources that they apply to, see Amazon Polly API Permissions: Actions, Permissions, and Resources Reference.

Specifying Conditions in a Policy

When you grant permissions, you can use the access policy language to specify the conditions when a policy should take effect. For example, you might want a policy to be applied only after a specific date. For more information about specifying conditions in a policy language, see Condition in the *IAM User Guide*.

To express conditions, you use predefined condition keys. There are no condition keys specific to Amazon Polly. However, there are AWS-wide condition keys that you can use as appropriate. For a complete list of AWS-wide keys, see Available Keys for Conditions in the *IAM User Guide*.

Using Identity-Based Policies (IAM Policies) for Amazon Polly

This topic provides examples of identity-based policies that demonstrate how an account administrator can attach permissions policies to IAM identities (that is, users, groups, and roles) and thereby grant permissions to perform operations on Amazon Polly resources.

Important
We recommend that you first review the introductory topics that explain the basic concepts and options available to manage access to your Amazon Polly resources. For more information, see Overview of Managing Access Permissions to Your Amazon Polly Resources.

- Permissions Required to Use the Amazon Polly Console
- AWS Managed (Predefined) Policies for Amazon Polly
- Customer Managed Policy Examples

The following shows an example of a permissions policy.

```
1  {
2      "Version": "2012-10-17",
3      "Statement": [{
4        "Sid": "AllowGet-Delete-ListActions",
5        "Effect": "Allow",
6        "Action": [
7           "polly:GetLexicon",
8           "polly:DeleteLexicon",
9           "polly:ListLexicons"],
10       "Resource": "*"
11        }
12    ],
13      "Statement": [{
14      "Sid": "NoOverrideMyLexicons",
15      "Effect": "Deny",
16      "Action": [
17         "polly:PutLexicon"],
18      "Resource": "arn:aws:polly:us-east-2:123456789012:lexicon/my*"
19        }
20    ]
21  }
```

The policy has two statements:

- The first statement grants permission for three Polly actions (`polly:GetLexicon`, `polly:DeleteLexicon`, and `polly:ListLexicons` on any lexicon. Use of the wildcard character (*) as the resource grants universal permissions for these actions across all regions and lexicons owned by this account.

- The second statement explicitly denies permission for one Polly action (`polly:PutLexicon`). The ARN shown as the resource specifically applies this permission all lexicons that begin with the letters "my" that are in the region `us-east-2`.

For a table showing all of the Amazon Polly API operations and the resources that they apply to, see Amazon Polly API Permissions: Actions, Permissions, and Resources Reference.

Permissions Required to Use the Amazon Polly Console

For a user to work with the Amazon Polly console, that user must have a minimum set of permissions that allows users to describe the Amazon Polly resources in their AWS account.

If you create an IAM policy that is more restrictive than the minimum required permissions, the console won't function as intended for users with that IAM policy.

You don't need to allow minimum console permissions for users that are making calls only to the AWS CLI or the Amazon Polly API.

To use the Amazon Polly console, you need to grant permissions to all the Amazon Polly APIs. There are no additional permissions needed. The following permissions policy is all that is needed to use the Amazon Polly console.

```
1  }
2  "Version": "2012-10-17",
3     "Statement": [{
4        "Sid": "Console-AllowAllPollyActions",
5        "Effect": "Allow",
6        "Action": [
7           "polly:*"],
8        "Resource": "*"
9        }
10    ]
11 }
```

AWS Managed (Predefined) Policies for Amazon Polly

AWS addresses many common use cases by providing standalone IAM policies that are created and administered by AWS. These AWS managed policies grant necessary permissions for common use cases so that you can avoid having to investigate what permissions are needed. For more information, see AWS Managed Policies in the *IAM User Guide*.

The following AWS managed policies, which you can attach to users in your account, are specific to Amazon Polly:

- **AmazonPollyReadOnlyAccess** – Grants read only access to resources, allows listing lexicons, fetching lexicons, listing available voices and synthesizing speech (including, applying lexicons to the synthesized speech).

- **AmazonPollyFullAccess** – Grants full access to resources and all the supported operations.

Note
You can review these permissions policies by signing in to the IAM console and searching for specific policies there.

You can also create your own custom IAM policies to allow permissions for Amazon Polly actions and resources. You can attach these custom policies to the IAM users or groups that require those permissions.

Customer Managed Policy Examples

In this section, you can find example user policies that grant permissions for various Amazon Polly actions. These policies work when you are using AWS SDKs or the AWS CLI. When you are using the console, you need to grant permissions to all the Amazon Polly APIs. This is discussed in Permissions Required to Use the Amazon Polly Console.

Note
All examples use the us-east-2 region and contain fictitious account IDs.

- Example 1: Allow All Amazon Polly Actions
- Example 2: Allow All Polly Actions Except DeleteLexicon

- Example 3: Allow DeleteLexicon
- Example 4: Allow Delete Lexicon in a Specified Region
- Example 5: Allow DeleteLexicon for Specified Lexicon

Example 1: Allow All Amazon Polly Actions

After you sign up (see Step 1.1: Sign up for AWS) you create an administrator user to manage your account, including creating users and managing their permissions.

You might choose to create a user who has permissions for all Amazon Polly actions (think of this user as a service-specific administrator) for working with Amazon Polly. You can attach the following permissions policy to this user.

```
1  {
2      "Version": "2012-10-17",
3      "Statement": [{
4          "Sid": "AllowAllPollyActions",
5          "Effect": "Allow",
6          "Action": [
7              "polly:*"],
8          "Resource": "*"
9          }
10     ]
11 }
```

Example 2: Allow All Polly Actions Except DeleteLexicon

The following permissions policy grants the user permissions to perform all actions except DeleteLexicon, with the permissions for delete explicitly denied in all regions.

```
1  {
2      "Version": "2012-10-17",
3      "Statement": [{
4          "Sid": "AllowAllActions-DenyDelete",
5          "Effect": "Allow",
6          "Action": [
7              "polly:DescribeVoices",
8              "polly:GetLexicon",
9              "polly:PutLexicon",
10             "polly:SynthesizeSpeech",
11             "polly:ListLexicons"],
12         "Resource": "*"
13         }
14         {
15         "Sid": "DenyDeleteLexicon",
16         "Effect": "Deny",
17         "Action": [
18             "polly:DeleteLexicon"],
19         "Resource": "*"
20         }
21     ]
22 }
```

Example 3: Allow DeleteLexicon

The following permissions policy grants the user permissions to delete any lexicon that you own regardless of the project or region in which it is located.

```
1  {
2    "Version": "2012-10-17",
3    "Statement": [{
4        "Sid": "AllowDeleteLexicon",
5        "Effect": "Allow",
6        "Action": [
7           "polly:DeleteLexicon"],
8        "Resource": "*"
9        }
10    ]
11 }
```

Example 4: Allow Delete Lexicon in a Specified Region

The following permissions policy grants the user permissions to delete any lexicon in any project that you own that is located in a single region (in this case, us-east-2).

```
1  {
2    "Version": "2012-10-17",
3    "Statement": [{
4        "Sid": "AllowDeleteSpecifiedRegion",
5        "Effect": "Allow",
6        "Action": [
7           "polly:DeleteLexicon"],
8        "Resource": "arn:aws:polly:us-east-2:123456789012:lexicon/*"
9        }
10    ]
11 }
```

Example 5: Allow DeleteLexicon for Specified Lexicon

The following permissions policy grants the user permissions to delete a specific lexicon that you own (in this case, myLexicon) in a specific region (in this case, us-east-2).

```
1  {
2    "Version": "2012-10-17",
3    "Statement": [{
4        "Sid": "AllowDeleteForSpecifiedLexicon",
5        "Effect": "Allow",
6        "Action": [
7           "polly:DeleteLexicon"],
8        "Resource": "arn:aws:polly:us-east-2:123456789012:lexicon/myLexicon"
9        }
10    ]
11 }
```

Amazon Polly API Permissions: Actions, Permissions, and Resources Reference

When you are setting up Access Control and writing a permissions policy that you can attach to an IAM identity (identity-based policies), you can use the following table as a reference. The table lists each Amazon Polly API operation, the corresponding actions for which you can grant permissions to perform the action, and the AWS resource for which you can grant the permissions. You specify the actions in the policy's `Action` field, and you specify the resource value in the policy's `Resource` field.

You can use AWS-wide condition keys in your Amazon Polly policies to express conditions. For a complete list of AWS-wide keys, see Available Keys in the *IAM User Guide*.

Note
To specify an action, use the `polly` prefix followed by the API operation name (for example, `polly:GetLexicon`).

If you see an expand arrow () in the upper-right corner of the table, you can open the table in a new window. To close the window, choose the close button (**X**) in the lower-right corner.

Amazon Polly API and Required Permissions for Actions

Amazon Polly API Operations	Required Permissions (API Actions)	Resources
DeleteLexicon	polly:DeleteLexicon	`arn:aws:polly:region :account-id:lexicon/ LexiconName`
DescribeVoices	polly:DescribeVoices	`*`
GetLexicon	polly:GetLexicon	`arn:aws:polly:region :account-id:lexicon/ LexiconName`
ListLexicons	polly:ListLexicons	`arn:aws:polly:region: account-id:lexicon/*`
PutLexicon	polly:PutLexicon	`*`
SynthesizeSpeech	polly:SynthesizeSpeech	`*`

Amazon Polly supports Identity-based policies for actions at the resource-level. Therefore, the `Resource` value is indicated by the ARN. For example: `arn:aws:polly:us-east-2:account-id:lexicon/*` as the `Resource` value specifies permissions on all owned lexicons within the `us-east-2`region.

Because Amazon Polly doesn't support permissions for actions at the resource-level, most policies specify a wildcard character (*) as the `Resource` value. However, if it is necessary to limit permissions to a specific region this wildcard character is replaced with the appropriate ARN: `arn:aws:polly:region:account-id:lexicon/*`.

Document History for Amazon Polly

The following table describes the documentation for this release of Amazon Polly.

- **Latest documentation update: **April 19, 2017

Change	Description	Date
New service and guide	This is the initial release of the AWS Text-to-Speech service, Amazon Polly, and the Amazon Polly Developer Guide.	November 30, 2016
New feature and expanded documentation	This is an update to Amazon Polly, and includes the new Speech Marks feature as well as an expansion of SSML capabilities.	April 19, 2017
Two new voices, new language, and expended regions	This is an update to Amazon Polly, and includes the following: [See the AWS documentation website for more details]	November 15, 2017

AWS Glossary

For the latest AWS terminology, see the AWS Glossary in the *AWS General Reference*.

www.ingramcontent.com/pod-product-compliance
Lightning Source LLC
LaVergne TN
LVHW082038050326
832904LV00005B/230